The Believer's
AUTHORITY
STUDY GUIDE

KENNETH E. HAGIN

The Believer's
AUTHORITY
STUDY GUIDE

KENNETH E. HAGIN

29 28 27 26 25 24 23   13 12 11 10 09 08 07

The Believer's Authority Study Guide
ISBN-13: 978-0-89276-545-4
ISBN-10: 0-89276-545-3

Copyright © 2014 Rhema Bible Church
AKA Kenneth Hagin Ministries, Inc.
Printed in the USA

In the U.S. write:
Kenneth Hagin Ministries
P.O. Box 50126
Tulsa, OK 74150-0126
1-888-28-FAITH
rhema.org

In Canada write:
Kenneth Hagin Ministries of Canada
P.O. Box 335, Station D
Etobicoke (Toronto), Ontario
Canada M9A 4X3
1-866-70-RHEMA
rhemacanada.org

Contents

Introduction

One of the most important truths we as believers can know is the authority we have in Christ. Jesus transferred this authority to us before He ascended into Heaven. When we understand this authority and begin operating in it, our lives will be transformed. No longer will we have to be in bondage to the enemy. No matter what attack the devil brings against us, we can come out of it victorious through Christ.

This study guide is designed to be used with the book *The Believer's Authority: Legacy Edition* and two audio teaching sets, *The Believer's Authority* and the *Reigning in Life as a King Series*. Although you can work through this material by yourself, we believe you will receive the most benefit through group study. Discussion and interaction with others can add to what you glean from these lessons.

Each lesson in this study guide contains the following:

Instructions

The instructions at the beginning of each lesson tell you which audio teaching to listen to and which chapters of the book to read.

Lesson Overview

The Lesson Overview is a summary of what is taught in each lesson. It's a recap of the main points of what you'll want to know.

Fill-in-the-Blank Questions

The fill-in-the-blank questions are primarily taken from the book. Don't be concerned about coming up with the exact word. It's more important that you get the concept of what the question is asking. All of the answers are in the Answer Key at the back of the book.

Multiple-Choice Questions

The multiple-choice questions are primarily taken from the audio teachings. Circle the correct answer to each question. The answers are listed in the Answer Key.

Questions for Personal Reflection

We've also included questions for personal reflection and/or discussion. These give you an opportunity to think about how you can apply the principles taught in the study guide to your life.

Bonus Material

At the end of each lesson is a brief teaching that is not covered in the textbook or in the audio recordings. It's bonus material that reinforces the point that each believer has authority in Christ.

Thoughts for Group Facilitators

As a group facilitator, you can make it easier for others to learn about their authority in Christ. Here are a few ideas to help you be a more effective leader:

- Open and close the sessions with prayer.

- Make sure that you've gone through each lesson's assignment and have answered all questions. By completing the study guide lesson ahead of time, you will be better able to guide others through it.

- Make sure that all participants have *The Believer's Authority: Legacy Edition* book, the study guide, and the two sets of audio teachings.

- After the group members have completed each study guide chapter at home, it may help to begin the session by going through the "Fill-in-the-Blank Questions" and "Multiple-Choice Questions" as a group. This way, you can make sure your group members have grasped the material. During this review, ask different ones to provide answers as a way to get everyone involved. Remember: having the right idea or concept is more important than having exactly the right word.

- It's good to have group members share their thoughts from the "Questions for Personal Reflection" section. If you have a large group, it can help to have them break up into smaller groups of five or six people to do this.

The Believer's Authority

— ·◦· —

Study Guide

Lesson One

Lesson Overview

Some Christians become fearful whenever the devil or demons are mentioned. They'll even lower their voices to a whisper when talking about them. Others take an opposite stance and feel that it's their responsibility to "wrestle" against principalities and powers. The truth is, neither group really understands the authority Jesus gave them over Satan and his demonic forces. They don't know they don't have to be afraid of the devil *or* "war" against the forces of darkness.

Jesus defeated Satan through His death at Calvary. During His three days in hell, Jesus conquered the devil and all of his demonic forces. He also took the keys of hell and death from

Satan (Rev. 1:18). Before Jesus ascended into Heaven, He transferred His authority over the devil and demonic powers to *every* believer, not just to a few select Christians or to those called to the five-fold ministry. (See Matt. 28:18–20 and Mark 16:15–18.)

This authority belongs to us whether we realize it or not. Satan doesn't want us to learn about the authority we have over him and will do everything he can to hide this truth from us. He will fight believers more on this subject than on any other truth. If he is able to blind our eyes to our authority, he can easily defeat us in every area of our lives.

Once we know that we have authority over our enemy, it's up to us to exercise, or enforce, that authority. It doesn't work automatically. Simply knowing that we have authority over Satan is not enough. If we don't *use* it, we are allowing the devil to dominate us. Only knowledge that is acted upon will bring results.

Because Jesus triumphed over Satan, we don't have to "war" against our enemy. Our combat with the devil should be from the viewpoint that Jesus Christ has already defeated him. Our battle, so to speak, is simply enforcing what Christ has already won for us. Satan can't dominate us unless we allow him to. When we realize this and walk in our authority, we will enjoy the reality of what is rightfully ours and face the devil without any fear or hesitancy.

Fill-in-the-Blank Questions

1. Jesus transferred His _____ to the Church.

2. We must _____ on the Word for it to work for us. It doesn't work _____.

This authority is not the property of only a few people. It's the true possession of every child of God.

~ Scriptures ~

EPHESIANS 1:16–17

16 [I] cease not to give thanks for you, making mention of you in my prayers;

17 That the God of our Lord Jesus Christ, the Father of glory, may give unto you the spirit of wisdom and revelation in the knowledge of him.

3. The devil _____ dominate us unless we _____ him to.

4. It's knowing the _____ that sets us free.

5. Many Christians have tried to do through _____ what only _____ _____ will do.

6. According to Ephesians 6:10, we are to be strong in the _____ and not in _____.

7. Christianity is the only religion in the world in which the God we worship lives _____ us.

8. The _____ we have as believers belongs to us whether we know it or not.

9. If Christians have problems in their lives, it's because they have not _____ their authority and have _____ problems to exist.

10. Authority is delegated _____.

Multiple-Choice Questions

1. If Christians don't know they have authority over the devil,

   a. Jesus will use His authority on their behalf.

   b. It doesn't matter. Satan does not bother people who are born again.

   c. The devil will take advantage of their ignorance and dominate their lives.

   d. It will still automatically manifest in their lives.

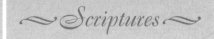
Scriptures

EPHESIANS 3:14–17

14 For this cause I bow my knees unto the Father of our Lord Jesus Christ,

15 Of whom the whole family in heaven and earth is named,

16 That he would grant you, according to the riches of his glory, to be strengthened with might by his Spirit in the inner man;

17 That Christ may dwell in your hearts by faith.

Knowledge acted upon brings results.

The value of authority depends upon the force behind the user. God Himself is the force behind [our] authority.

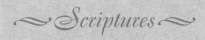

~ Scriptures ~

EPHESIANS 1:3 (ASV)

3 Blessed be the God

and Father of our

Lord Jesus Christ,

who hath blessed us

with every spiritual

blessing in the

heavenly places

in Christ.

2. What sets people free?

 a. Prayer

 b. Fasting

 c. The truth of the Word

 d. Both a and b

3. The value of authority depends on what?

 a. The power behind it

 b. Whether we have sin in our lives

 c. How many Bible verses we have memorized

 d. How big our offerings are

4. When we are in a crisis, where should we look for help?

 a. We should call the prayer line of every major ministry.

 b. We should call our pastor—no matter what time it is.

 c. We should contact the most spiritual person in our church.

 d. We should look to the Greater One Who dwells in our hearts.

5. Can we exercise authority over another person's will?

 a. Yes, we can exercise authority over any person's will, whether we know the individual or not.

 b. No, we are only able to exercise authority over spirits, not people.

 c. Yes, we can exercise authority over the wills of our family members.

 d. Yes, we can dominate people who have meek temperaments.

Questions for Personal Reflection

1. In what ways have you used the authority Jesus delegated to you? Are there areas of your life where you have not used your authority as a believer? What practical steps can you take so you always operate in the authority you have been given?

2. In what areas of your life has the devil been able to dominate you? How did you learn to stand against the devil in these areas? How has your life changed since you began acting on the Word?

3. Have there been times in your life when you tried to be strong in yourself instead of getting your strength from the Lord as instructed in Ephesians 6:10? What practical steps can you take to rely on the Lord instead of on yourself?

4. When you are thoroughly conscious of the authority you have as a believer and the divine power that stands behind that authority, you can face the enemy without any fear or hesitancy. How are you doing in applying this truth to your life? Have there been times when you were filled with fear in a situation? What did you do to put your full trust in God?

5. Are there times when you look to Heaven for help instead of looking to the Holy Spirit Who resides inside you? Which scriptures show you that God is *in* you? What practical steps can you take to remember that the answer to all of your needs lies within you?

6. Are you building the truths of the believer's authority into your spirit? What can you do to develop in these truths?

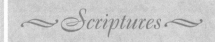

Scriptures

EPHESIANS 6:12

12 For we wrestle not against flesh and blood, but against principalities, against powers, against the rulers of the darkness of this world, against spiritual wickedness in high places.

The power that's behind us is the Greater One Who's in us.

7. How often do you give up when your circumstances don't change immediately? What can you do to keep from quitting?

8. Review the scriptures in this lesson. Which one speaks to you the most? Why?

9. Read the quotes in this lesson. Which one is the most meaningful to you? Why?

10. What is one truth you learned from this lesson that you can apply to your life? How will it enhance your life?

BONUS MATERIAL

Knowing What's Ours

Many Christians don't know what belongs to them in Christ. As a result, they keep trying to get what God has already provided for them. When they keep asking God for something that He has already given them, they are stepping out of faith. And when they're not in faith, they're not pleasing God, because the Bible says, *"Without faith it is impossible to please him"* (Heb. 11:6).

Our wonderful Heavenly Father has given us everything we need to be rich and strong. In God's great redemptive work, Jesus didn't do anything for Himself. He did it all for us. Colossians 1:13 says that God *"hath delivered us from the power of*

The believer who is thoroughly conscious of the divine power behind him and of his own authority can face the enemy without fear or hesitancy.

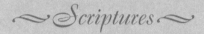

Scriptures

LUKE 10:19

19 Behold, I give

unto you power

to tread on serpents

and scorpions,

and over all the

power of the enemy:

and nothing

shall by any means

hurt you.

darkness, and hath translated us into the kingdom of his dear Son." Our spirits were translated into God's Kingdom the moment we were born again.

Christians often ask fellow believers, "Pray that I'll be delivered from . . . ." But Colossians 1:13 tells us that we have *already* been delivered from the power of darkness and have been translated into the Kingdom of God's dear Son. The word *translate* means "to remove from one place and put into another." Born-again Christians have been removed from the power and authority of darkness and put into God's Kingdom. The word *darkness* refers to Satan and everything that is in his kingdom.

In Ephesians 4:27 we are told, *"Neither give place to the devil."* "You" is the understood subject of this verse. It's up to *you* not to give the devil any place. That means the devil can't take any place in our lives unless we allow him to. But that also means he can if we let him. So many Christians don't know they have authority over the devil and unknowingly yield to him. Anytime they don't stand in their authority, the devil takes advantage of the situation and steps in to devour.

God's love for us is too great for Him to save us, make us new creatures in Christ, bring the Church of Christ into existence, and then leave us to contend with the devil in our own strength. After Jesus defeated Satan and his demonic forces, He transferred His authority to the Church before He ascended into Heaven (Matt. 28:18–20; Mark 16:15–18).

Ephesians 1:3 tells us that we have been blessed *"with all spiritual blessings in heavenly places in Christ."* Through Christ, we are fully equipped to be victorious over the devil. Christians should not be ruled by demons and evil spirits. Knowing who we are in Christ and using the authority we have been given enables us to overcome any attack of the devil.

~ *Scriptures* ~

EPHESIANS 6:10

10 Finally, my brethren, be strong in the Lord, and in the power of his might.

I am never without help because I am never without God.

Satan no longer has authority over us, and he cannot dominate us when we stand our ground and operate in our authority. So let's rise up and use what is ours. Through the blood of Christ, the Name of Jesus, and the Word of God, we have everything we need to be victorious whenever our adversary tries to lift his ugly head.

(Editor's Note: This article has been adapted from a message Kenneth E. Hagin taught on April 18, 1988, during a Spring Satellite Seminar.*)*

Lives will be revolutionized when we realize the authority that belongs to Christ belongs to each member of the Body of Christ.

The Believer's Authority
Study Guide

Lesson Two

Instructions

- Read chapter 2, "What Is Authority?," from the textbook *The Believer's Authority: Legacy Edition.*

- Listen to the message "Exercising Our Authority" from *The Believer's Authority* audio series.

- Work through this lesson.

Lesson Overview

It's amazing how many Christians are afraid of the devil. In a sense, they've been taught to be afraid of him. In some churches, preachers always talk about the devil. And a lot of believers constantly talk about the devil doing this and the devil doing that. It's no wonder people think the devil has more power than God! They've forgotten that Jesus stripped Satan of his power and authority.

First Peter 5:8 says that *"the devil, as a roaring lion, walketh about, seeking whom he may devour."* But Scripture also tells us that if we resist the devil, he *will* flee from us (James 4:7). Satan is actually afraid of Christians who know their rights and walk in their God-given authority. He is well aware of the power that backs up born-again believers. The only way the devil can dominate believers is to trick them into believing that he is more powerful than he actually is. Unfortunately, too many Christians fall for the deceptions of the devil and allow him to push them around.

The value of any authority depends on the force behind it. God Himself is the force behind our authority. When we are thoroughly conscious of the divine power behind us, we will never again allow the devil to have supremacy in our lives. Instead we will face Satan and his demonic kingdom without fear or hesitancy.

The power of Heaven not only stands behind us; that power is also *in* us. First John 4:4 says, *"Greater is he that is in you, than he that is in the world."* It is vital that we realize our position in Christ—who we are and what we have in Him. Then it's up to us to exercise the authority He has given us. As we believe and meditate on that truth, it will become a part of our inner consciousness. The devil has been walking on us far too long. It's time that we start walking on him!

Fill-in-the-Blank Questions

1. We have been _____ _____ _____ with Christ (Eph. 2:6).

2. Praying that God will rebuke the devil is a _____ of time.

3. If we resist the devil, he will _____ _____ us (James 4:7).

4. Kenneth E. Hagin's definition of *flee* was _____ _____.

> *Even though Jesus overcame the devil for you, if you don't exercise that authority, the enemy, in everyday combat, will overcome you!*

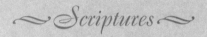

∽ Scriptures ∽

I PETER 5:8–9

8 Be sober, be vigilant; because your adversary the devil, as a roaring lion, walketh about, seeking whom he may devour:

9 Whom resist stedfast in the faith. . . .

5. Some people have more faith in _____ _____ than in _____.

6. We are to be strong in the power of _____ might, not in the power of _____ _____.

7. Every believer has the _____ _____ that Paul had in Christ Jesus.

8. The devil can't _____ any place in your life unless you _____ it to him.

9. Jesus has _____ everything He is going to do about the _____.

10. Satan cannot _____ you anymore.

Multiple-Choice Questions

1. How do you give place to the devil?

   a. Through fear

   b. Through lack of action

   c. By giving up and not standing your ground

   d. All of the above

2. What is the power behind our authority in Christ?

   a. The archangels Michael and Gabriel

   b. God Himself

   c. The amount of time we spend in prayer and Bible study

   d. All of the above

Scriptures

EPHESIANS 1:19–23

19 . . . according to the working of his mighty power,

20 Which he wrought in Christ, when he raised him from the dead, and set him at his own right hand in the heavenly places,

21 Far above all principality, and power, and might, and dominion, and every name that is named, not only in this world, but also in that which is to come:

22 And hath put all things under his feet, and gave him to be the head over all things to the church,

23 Which is his body, the fulness of him that filleth all in all.

3. Who is responsible to cast out demons?

   a. Every born-again believer

   b. Only the pastor of a church

   c. God. We are to pray and ask Him to do it.

   d. Angels. They are ministering spirits and they will cast out devils if we ask them to.

4. When the devil raises his ugly head, what should you do?

   a. Get your closest friend to agree with you that the devil won't be able to harm you.

   b. Turn the situation over to God.

   c. Resist him and use your authority in Christ.

   d. Hide until he leaves.

5. What are you as a Christian supposed to rule and reign over?

   a. Disease

   b. Poverty

   c. Everything that would hinder you in your individual life

   d. All of the above

Questions for Personal Reflection

1. Do you recognize the difference between *power* and *authority*? Have you ever tried to resist the devil in your own power instead of the authority you have in Christ? What happened?

2. In your personal life, have you been able to overcome the devil day after day? If yes, what is enabling you to be victorious? If no, what can you do to change that?

Authority is yours whether you feel like it or not. But YOU must exercise it. Nobody else can exercise that authority for you.

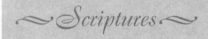

Scriptures

EPHESIANS 2:6

6 And hath raised us up together, and made us sit together in heavenly places in Christ Jesus.

3. Why do you think spiritual things don't work automatically? What advantage or disadvantage is there to this? Why do you think people *want* spiritual things to happen automatically?

4. James 4:7 says, *"Resist the devil, and he will flee from you."* How are you applying this truth to your life? How have you successfully resisted the devil? What can you do that will better help you resist him?

5. Why do you think some people have more faith in the devil's power than in God's power? What can be done to change this?

6. Has the devil ever gained a foothold in your life? If so, were you able to exercise your authority over him and force him to leave? How did you do that? What steps are you taking so he doesn't gain another foothold?

7. Have you ever given place to the devil? What happened? What can you do so you don't give the devil an opportunity to work in your life?

8. Review the scriptures in this lesson. Which one speaks to you the most? Why?

9. Read the quotes in this lesson. Which one is the most meaningful to you? Why?

10. What one truth have you learned from this lesson that you can apply to your life? How will it improve your life?

Scriptures

MATTHEW 28:18–19

18 And Jesus came and spake unto them, saying, All power is given unto me in heaven and in earth.

19 Go ye therefore, and teach all nations, baptizing them in the name of the Father, and of the Son, and of the Holy Ghost.

I don't have any faith in [the devil's] power at all. I've got faith in the power of God.

God's plan is for you, the individual Christian, to rule and reign as a king in YOUR life.

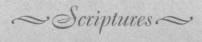

COLOSSIANS 1:13

13 Who hath delivered us

from the power

of darkness,

and hath translated us

into the kingdom

of his dear Son.

BONUS MATERIAL

Possessing What Is Ours

Everything Christ obtained for mankind through His redemptive work on the cross belongs to believers everywhere. Unfortunately, many Christians do not realize the scope of what Jesus has purchased for them. Ephesians 1:3 says that God has *"blessed us with all spiritual blessings in heavenly places in Christ."* Not only is eternal life ours, but so are healing, strength, light, and wisdom, as well as supply and sufficiency. We only have to receive what Jesus paid so dearly for with His shed blood.

Christians have a lot of possessions available to them that they do not take advantage of. We see this so clearly with healing. Many folks know that Jesus healed in the Bible, but they don't believe healing is available to Christians today. Others think that God sometimes withholds His healing touch from some so they will "learn a lesson." And some people simply don't know that healing is available to them.

We can't possess something that we don't know is ours—that we don't know we have a right to. And we won't resist sickness if we believe God put it on us. Sickness is not from God; it is from Satan. It has never been a "tool" that God uses to teach His children something. The devil comes to steal, kill, and destroy (John 10:10). God wants us to have a full life—one in which we live in health. When we fully understand what belongs to us as children of God and we comprehend the authority we have been given, we will never again allow sickness to rule over us.

Jesus became our Lord and Savior when we were born again. At that moment we were rescued from the power of darkness and brought into the Kingdom of God's Son (Col. 1:13). When we speak of darkness, we are referring to the kingdom of Satan, which includes sin, sickness, disease, and everything else that is evil. The devil no longer has authority over us. In fact, it's just the other way around. We have authority over the devil and all the hosts of darkness.

Unfortunately, many Christians allow the devil to dominate them in the area of sickness. Although Jesus obtained healing for us more than 2,000 years ago, some Christians accept any sickness that tries to come on them. If we will resist the devil, use our authority in Christ, and receive what has already been bought for us, we can live free from sickness and disease.

(*Editor's Note: This article has been adapted from a lesson Kenneth E. Hagin taught during a* Spring Satellite Seminar *on April 19, 1988.*)

Scriptures

I JOHN 4:4

4 Ye are of God, little children, and have overcome them: because greater is he that is in you, than he that is in the world.

[Authority] doesn't work automatically.

The Believer's Authority

—◦•◦—

Study Guide

Lesson Three

Lesson Overview

Paul's prayer for the church at Ephesus was that they would know and understand the greatness of God's power. That power was demonstrated in the raising of Jesus from the dead. Satan and his cohorts tried to oppose the resurrection of Christ. But Jesus defeated all the forces of hell and *"made a shew of them openly"* (Col. 2:15).

In ancient times, victorious kings paraded their captives through the streets so citizens would know of the fallen king's overthrow. After Satan was defeated, he was displayed as a defeated foe in three worlds: Heaven, hell, and earth. Satan's downfall is recorded in Scripture so we would know of his defeat and not allow him to dominate us.

[Christ's] triumph is my triumph because I arose with Him. I'm seated with Him there at the place of authority.

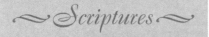

Scriptures

COLOSSIANS 1:15–16

15 [Jesus] is the image of the invisible God, the firstborn of every creature:

16 For by him were all things created, that are in heaven, and that are in earth, visible and invisible, whether they be thrones, or dominions, or principalities, or powers: all things were created by him, and for him:

When Jesus rose from the dead, mankind was raised up with Him. And when Christ ascended to Heaven and sat down at the right hand of the Father, we sat down with Him. Before Christ we were spiritually dead in sin. But we were made alive with Christ and made to sit together in heavenly places in Him (Eph. 2:5–6). The elevation of the Body of Christ into the heavenlies clearly points out that we share not only Christ's throne but also His authority.

The Church has failed to see that Jesus is entirely dependent upon believers to carry out His plans on the earth. Although the right hand of God is the center of power in the universe, neither God nor Jesus is going to enforce the victory that Christ wrought over the devil. Jesus delegated that responsibility to the Church. We were not left powerless in our fight against the devil. Jesus gave us His authority, His Name, and His blood. And with these weapons, we have everything we need to enforce Christ's victory on the earth.

Many times people ask, "Why do bad things happen?" Often we haven't used our authority when we should have. We haven't stood in the power and authority we have in Christ and enforced God's plan in our lives and on the earth. However, when we recognize who we are in Christ, our lives will be revolutionized.

Fill-in-the-Blank Questions

1. Jesus is seated at the right hand of the Father, which is the _____ of _____.

2. Raising Jesus from the dead was the _____ work of God ever recorded.

3. Jesus put the devil's defeat on display in three places: _____, _____, and _____.

4. The source of our authority is found in the _____ and seating of Christ at the right hand of God.

5. There is _____ in death.

6. According to First Corinthians 6:17, we are _____ with Christ.

7. God wants _____ Christians to exercise authority over the powers of the air.

8. God expects Christians to do _____ works than what Jesus did while He was here on the earth.

9. A better translation of the word *power* in the *King James Version* of Matthew 28:18 would be _____.

10. When Christ was raised from the dead, all of _____ was also raised from the dead.

Multiple-Choice Questions

1. How can a believer control an adverse situation?

   a. The person who is the loudest and pushiest controls any situation.

   b. The believer who knows and acts on his rights, privileges, and authority in Christ can control how a situation turns out.

   c. God will step in and take control of the situation when you beg Him to.

   d. None of the above. People don't have any control over how things turn out—whatever happens, happens.

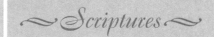

Scriptures

COLOSSIANS 1:17–20

17 And he is before all things, and by him all things consist.

18 And he is the head of the body, the church: who is the beginning, the firstborn from the dead; that in all things he might have the preeminence.

19 For it pleased the Father that in him should all fulness dwell;

20 And, having made peace through the blood of his cross, by him to reconcile all things unto himself; by him, I say, whether they be things in earth, or things in heaven.

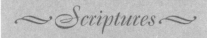

*There is victory
even in death.*

~Scriptures~

COLOSSIANS 2:3–5

3 In whom are hid all the

treasures of wisdom

and knowledge.

4 And this I say, lest any

man should beguile you

with enticing words.

5 For though I be absent in

the flesh, yet am I with you

in the spirit, joying and

beholding your order,

and the stedfastness of

your faith in Christ.

2. In the message "Our Place of Authority" from *The Believer's Authority* audio series, Kenneth E. Hagin states, "You can pray and not really exercise authority." How do Christians do this?

   a. Christians are not operating in authority when they try to be strong in themselves. Their strength comes from the Lord.

   b. Christians are not operating in authority when they try to go head-to-head with the devil in prayer combat.

   c. Christians are not operating in authority when their prayers are filled with doubt and they beg and plead with God to move on their behalf.

   d. All of the above

3. How does God carry out His plans on the earth?

   a. God's plans will automatically come to pass regardless of what people do.

   b. God resorts to using the wicked because He can't get Christians to cooperate with Him.

   c. God is dependent upon the Church to carry out His commands and exercise authority.

   d. God has always had a small remnant of people who will intercede until His plans are brought forth on the earth.

4. What does God consider our reasonable service to Him (Rom. 12:1)?

   a. We are to present our bodies to Him.

   b. We are to always pay our tithes.

   c. We are to win someone to Christ at least once a month.

   d. We are to read at least one chapter of the Bible every day and pray in tongues for a minimum of an hour each day.

5. What does it mean to "keep our bodies under" (1 Cor. 9:27)?

    a. We are to exercise and stay in top physical condition.

    b. We pray and fast until we have dropped one clothing size.

    c. We allow our spirit man to dominate our bodies.

    d. We can't keep our bodies under. Only God can do that for us.

Personal Reflection Questions

1. What are your thoughts about being raised together with Christ and being seated with Him at God's right hand? Does knowing you are seated with Christ give you a different perspective of the devil and his activities in the earth?

2. Jesus paralyzed Satan and his demonic forces through His death and resurrection. Do you feel that the devil has been paralyzed in your life? If not, what can you do so you are not dominated by him anymore?

3. Jesus said that those who believe in Him would do the same works that He did, and even greater works (John 14:12). In what ways have you been doing the works of Christ? Are there areas of your life where you can improve? What do you think it will take for you to do the greater works that Jesus also talked about in John 14:12?

4. In examining your life, do you talk more about what the devil is doing than about how God defeated him through Jesus' death and resurrection? If you talk more about Satan's activities, what can you do to change the way you talk?

Scriptures

COLOSSIANS 2:6–7

6 As ye have therefore received Christ Jesus the Lord, so walk ye in him: 7 Rooted and built up in him, and stablished in the faith, as ye have been taught, abounding therein with thanksgiving.

We as a church have authority on the earth that we've never realized. We've only barely touched a little bit of it—barely gotten into the edge of it.

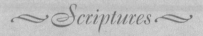

Heaven is going to back you up in whatever you do.

~ Scriptures ~

COLOSSIANS 2:12–13

12 Buried with him in baptism, wherein also ye are risen with him through the faith of the operation of God, who hath raised him from the dead.

13 And you, being dead in your sins and the uncircumcision of your flesh, hath he quickened together with him, having forgiven you all trespasses;

5. Are you reigning as a king in all areas of your life? Which areas could use some improvement? What practical steps can you take so you begin to reign as a king in *every* area of your life?

6. Have you ever had to plead a case with God for someone who was near death? What is the best way to plead someone's case? Why is it important to God that we die in the right way?

7. Do you see yourself seated with Christ in heavenly places? If not, what practical steps can you take to see yourself risen with Him? Why is it important that you see yourself this way?

8. Review the scriptures in this lesson. Which one speaks to you the most? Why?

9. Read the quotes in this lesson. Which one is the most meaningful to you? Why?

10. What is one truth you learned from this lesson that you can apply to your life? How will it enhance your life?

BONUS MATERIAL

The Devil Is Under Our Feet

Everything has been placed under Jesus' feet (Eph. 1:22). That includes the devil. Since we are a part of the Body of Christ, all things are under our feet as well. It doesn't matter what type of problem comes against us—physical, emotional, financial, family, and so forth—we can walk on top of every one of these situations.

Psalm 91:13 says, *"Thou shalt tread upon the lion and adder."* This verse uses lions and adders to represent forces that are strong and fierce. It is literally talking about Satan and his demonic host. If we're treading on something, it means we're walking on it. In this case, we are supposed to walk on devils and demons.

The word *adder* in Psalm 91:13 is also translated "asp," "serpent," and "cobra." Looking further at this word, we see that it carries with it the thought of a nest of snakes. Spiritually speaking, this is referring to different types of demons. But no matter how many demons we encounter, we have the authority to tread on *all* of them.

Deuteronomy 32:33 talks about the cruel venom of asps, and Romans 3:13 says, *"The poison of asps is under their lips."* These verses refer to backbiting, tale-bearing, and slandering. We have probably all experienced the vicious sting of untrue and unkind words spoken about us. When we become victims of poisonous words, we must remember that we have the power to tread on what was said. The unkind, cutting words of others don't have to hurt us. We can walk over the lies and keep going!

In a different vein of thought, failures and missteps in life can also sting. They can crush us and keep us from moving forward. We have authority to tread on the mistakes we've made. We can step over failures and rise up in victory through Christ.

God wants us to rule and reign in our lives. In other words, He wants us to experience victory all the time, not just occasionally. Although He has given us the victory, *we* must take possession of it. It's ours potentially. Unfortunately, that is as far as many believers get. They know God's blessings belong to them, but they never possess them. We have to put our foot down and demand that what God says about us is true. We are victorious, healthy, prosperous, and so forth.

God told Joshua, *"Every place that the sole of your foot shall tread upon, that have I given unto you"* (Joshua 1:3). God gave the

---

Scriptures

COLOSSIANS 2:14–15

14 Blotting out the handwriting of ordinances that was against us, which was contrary to us, and took it out of the way, nailing it to his cross;

15 And having spoiled principalities and powers, he made a shew of them openly, triumphing over them in it.

Promised Land to Joshua, but Joshua didn't possess the land until he took steps *to take* what was his. Many people say that they are waiting for God to give them the victory. He can't *give* them the victory because *they already have it*. He's waiting for them to "take" it. What Jesus did for us on the cross will never become a reality in our lives until we do something about it.

Many people are hoping that God will heal them. But He already provided healing for us through Jesus. God is waiting for us to "take" what Jesus bought for us. Too many people think the blessings of God will just fall on them. But we have to put forth some effort. "Thou shalt tread" means that *we* have to do something. We have to stand on the Word of God in faith until we see it become a reality in our lives.

How much victory we experience really depends on us. If we don't tread on sickness, disease, and poverty, we will remain sick and poor. It's up to us to put the devil on the run by using our authority, standing firm in our faith, and thanking God for what He has wrought for us. Scripture tells us that when we resist the devil, he *will* flee (James 4:7). When we enforce Christ's victory, we will receive everything that belongs to us!

(Editor's Note: This article has been adapted from a message Kenneth E. Hagin taught during Winter Bible Seminar *on February 16, 1997.)*

Read the Epistles and find out what happened to you— that you've been raised together with Him and you're now seated with Christ!

The Believer's Authority

—·•·—

Study Guide

Lesson Four

Instructions

- Read chapter 4, "Breaking the Power of the Devil," from the textbook *The Believer's Authority: Legacy Edition*.

- Listen to the message "Authority Over Fear" from *The Believer's Authority* audio series.

- Work through this lesson.

Lesson Overview

It was always God's plan for Adam to rule and reign over the earth. After God created Adam, He gave him dominion over the earth (Gen. 1:28). However, when Adam committed high treason and sold out to the devil by eating the forbidden fruit (Gen. 3:1–7), he lost his authority over the earth. He handed his dominion over to Satan, who then became "the god of this world" (2 Cor. 4:4). Although Jesus defeated the devil on the cross of Calvary, our enemy has a right to be on the earth until he is cast into the lake of fire and brimstone (Rev. 20:10).

Satan, however, doesn't have any right to dominate Christians. Jesus gave us *"power to tread on serpents and scorpions, and over ALL the power of the enemy"* (Luke 10:19). Believers can put a stop to the works of the devil by using their authority in Christ. If Christians would stand in faith and demand that God's promises be manifested in their lives, many of their problems would be solved. Many people, however, simply don't stand up and exercise their rights in Christ.

All too often, Christians are afraid of the devil. They have more faith in his power than in God's power. They don't realize that the Holy Spirit Who dwells in them is far greater than the defeated devil (1 John 4:4). When we fully understand that the Spirit of God dwells in us, we will be masters over the powers of darkness and everything they bring, including sickness, bondage, and torment.

Fill-in-the-Blank Questions

1. Fallen angels are _____ _____ who have been dethroned by the Lord Jesus Christ.

2. The authority Christ wrought for us is for _____, not sometime in the _____.

3. Because the devil has a right to be on the earth until Adam's lease runs out, he can rule over people *until* they are _____ _____.

4. Through Christ, Christians can _____ the devil.

5. Because _____ is not on the earth physically, all His authority has to be exercised through _____.

6. The Bible calls Jesus the _____ _____ Who became our substitute.

7. If the devil is able to keep us in the arena of _____ and _____, he will be able to whip us in every battle.

The thing that makes Christianity different from all other religions is the fact that Christianity is NOT a religion. It's a life!

∽ Scriptures ∽

JOHN 14:13–14

13 Whatsoever ye shall ask in my name, that will I do, that the Father may be glorified in the Son.

14 If ye shall ask any thing in my name, I will do it.

8. The most effective way to pray can be to _____ our rights of the devil.

9. John 14:13 says, *"Whatsoever ye shall ask in my name, that will I do."* The Greek word translated *ask* really means _____.

10. Our faith is based on the _____. If we don't see any change in our situation after using our authority, we should not be moved by what we _____.

Multiple-Choice Questions

1. What happens to us when the life of God is imparted into our spirits?

   a. Our spirit man is recreated and made new.

   b. God Himself moves in and takes up residence in our spirit being.

   c. We are made a master over the devil and the powers of darkness.

   d. All of the above

2. What makes Christianity different from all other religions?

   a. Jesus rose from the dead.

   b. The God we worship dwells in us.

   c. Christianity is not a religion. It's a life!

   d. All of the above

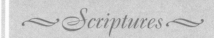
Scriptures

JOHN 16:23–24

23 In that day ye shall ask me nothing. Verily, verily, I say unto you, Whatsoever ye shall ask the Father in my name, he will give it you. 24 Hitherto have ye asked nothing in my name: ask, and ye shall receive, that your joy may be full.

We need to wake up and start living in the present tense and in the light and privileges of what belongs to us NOW!

The Church should be triumphant over ALL the power of the enemy.

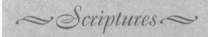

Scriptures

2 TIMOTHY 1:7

7 God hath not

given us

the spirit of fear;

but of power,

and of love,

and of

a sound mind.

3. What is the best way not to give in to fear?

   a. Pray in tongues for an hour before starting the day.

   b. Read Psalm 91 seven times a day.

   c. Quit talking fear.

   d. Bind and cast out the devil when we first sense fear.

4. How much power and authority does the Church have today?

   a. Over time, the power of God has diminished. The Church today has only a fraction of the power that the Early Church had.

   b. The Church today has the same amount of power that the Early Church had.

   c. The power of God increases over time. The Church today has more power than the Early Church.

   d. The power of God increases or decreases according to how long we pray in the Spirit.

5. If the Holy Spirit dwells in us, why do some Christians feel as though God is far away?

   a. They do not spend time with the Lord.

   b. They are more devil conscious than they are God conscious.

   c. They base their relationship with God solely on feelings.

   d. All of the above

Personal Reflection Questions

1. Are you convinced that Satan and his demonic forces have been defeated and are dethroned spirits? What can you do to remember that you have complete victory over the devil?

2. Why do you think the devil is able to dominate so many Christians? Do you ever try to get someone else to exercise authority over the devil on your behalf? What can you do so you know the devil will obey *your* words?

3. What can be the most effective way to pray when you exercise your authority over the devil? What should you do if you don't see any change in a situation after exercising your authority?

4. What did you receive when you received the life of God within your spirit? Are you walking in the light of that life? How have you taken advantage of what belongs to you?

5. Throughout the Old and New Testaments, we are told not to fear. How often do you give in to fear? What can you do so you don't fear? How often do you speak words of fear? What can you do so you don't talk fear?

6. In the message "Authority Over Fear" from *The Believer's Authority* audio series, Kenneth E. Hagin states that common sense teaches us that Jesus made us a master over the devil so we would reign as kings in life. Are you mastering the devil? Are you reigning as a king in life? If not, what steps can you take to do that?

Scriptures

LUKE 10:19

19 Behold, I give unto you power to tread on serpents and scorpions, and over all the power of the enemy: and nothing shall by any means hurt you.

I just wonder sometimes if we realize what we received when we received the life of God into our spirits, if we've ever really taken advantage of what belongs to us, if we've ever really walked in the light of that life.

~Scriptures~

ROMANS 5:17 (Amplified)

17 If because of one man's

trespass (lapse, offense)

death reigned through that

one, much more surely will

those who receive

[God's] overflowing grace

(unmerited favor) and the

free gift of righteousness

[putting them into right

standing with Himself] reign

as kings in life through the

one Man Jesus Christ

(the Messiah,

the Anointed One).

7. Do you understand that the Greater One dwells in you (1 John 4:4)? Do you ever feel that ministers can exercise their authority over the devil better than people who aren't called to full-time ministry? If so, why do you feel this way? What would it take for *you* to triumph over *all* the power of the devil?

8. Review the scriptures in this lesson. Which one speaks to you the most? Why?

9. Read the quotes in this lesson. Which one is the most meaningful to you? Why?

10. What is one truth you learned from this lesson that you can apply to your life? How will it enhance your life?

BONUS MATERIAL

The Blame Game

It's common to hear people ask, "Why did God permit this?" "Why doesn't God do something about this?" or, "Why did Jesus let that happen to me?" The answer may surprise you, but God can't do anything about it. It's up to the ones asking the question to exercise their authority in Christ and enforce the Word of God in their lives.

You see, Christ is the Head of the Church (Eph. 5:23) and we in the Church are His body (Eph. 5:30). Authority is conferred not only upon the Head but also upon the body. The same authority the Head has, the body has. Our head cannot do a thing without our body. In fact, our head can't do anything *except* through our body.

The same is true with Christ and the Church. Jesus is not here in a physical body, so it's up to the Church to enforce His will on the earth. Instead of doing this, many Christians don't do anything and blame God for what they are experiencing. It's not a matter of God letting bad things happen to them. *They've* actually allowed bad things to happen because they haven't accepted their responsibility and exercised their authority in Christ.

This is what happened in the Garden of Eden. We see clearly from the following passage that Adam never took responsibility for his actions.

GENESIS 3:8–12

8 They heard the voice of the Lord God walking in the garden in the cool of the day: and Adam and his wife hid themselves from the presence of the Lord God amongst the trees of the garden.

9 And the Lord God called unto Adam, and said unto him, Where art thou?

10 And he said, I heard thy voice in the garden, and I was afraid, because I was naked; and I hid myself.

11 And he said, Who told thee that thou wast naked? Hast thou eaten of the tree, whereof I commanded thee that thou shouldest not eat?

12 And the man said, The woman whom thou gavest to be with me, she gave me of the tree, and I did eat.

When God asked Adam if he ate the forbidden fruit, Adam immediately blamed Eve *and* God. Adam turned the situation around by saying, *"The woman whom thou gavest to be with me . . . ."* In other words, Adam was saying, "It's Your fault, God. You and the woman are to blame!"

People today aren't much different. It's a lot easier to blame someone else rather than place the blame where it belongs—squarely on our shoulders. Adversity comes to everybody. But God made provision for us to be overcomers. We can be victorious even in the most trying circumstances. It may feel as though our situation is beyond our control, but God has provided a way of escape from everything that comes against us. Our victory is found in His Word, the Name of Jesus, the blood of Jesus, and our authority in Christ.

Every Christian, really, is a master of the devil.

*Christians have the ability
to change things.*

We'd like to think we're not responsible for the adversity we encounter, whether it's sickness, financial lack, or some other trouble. But we are more responsible for what happens to us than many of us would like to admit. It's up to us to use what He has given us to change our circumstances.

We cannot allow ourselves to become so caught up in day-to-day affairs that we don't hear God's still, small voice when He tries to warn us and direct our paths to safety. We must be quick to use our authority when symptoms come on our bodies. And in adversity we must guard our lips and only speak words of faith.

When we realize that Christ's authority also belongs to each individual member of His Body, we will never be the same. We'll dominate the devil instead of letting him dominate us.

(*Editor's Note: This article has been adapted from the April 8, 1999, session of "The Believer's Authority" course Kenneth E. Hagin taught at Rhema Bible Training College.*)

The Believer's Authority
— ·•· —
Study Guide

Lesson Five

Lesson Overview

Christians know they need God, but many believe that God doesn't need them. They think that Jesus can get along without them. This sentiment is far from the truth. Jesus' death on the cross completely destroyed the power of the devil. But the victory of the cross will never be carried out on the earth apart from the Church.

There isn't any place in the New Testament where the Church is told to petition God or Jesus to do something about Satan. Jesus has done everything He is going to do about the devil until an angel binds him with a chain and puts him in the bottomless pit (Rev. 20:1–3). Unless the Body of Christ rises up in their authority and stops the works of the devil, nothing will be done.

Folks are trying to get somebody else to act for them. Act upon God's Word for yourself.

When the children of Israel were about to cross the Jordan River and enter the Promised Land, God told Joshua, *"Every place that the sole of your foot shall tread upon, that have I given unto you"* (Joshua 1:3). In essence, God was saying, "I'm going to give the land to you, but you have to possess it." The way we possess *our* land—what God has given us in His great plan of redemption—is by believing His Word, receiving it by faith, and enforcing its presence in our lives by using our authority in Christ.

Fill-in-the-Blank Questions

1. We help _____ carry out His work on the _____.

2. If we _____ our ground against the devil, he will _____.

3. God needs _____just as much as we need _____.

4. The work of God must be carried out through the _____ _____ _____.

5. We are seated _____ the powers of darkness.

6. The job of believers is to _____ Christ's victory.

7. If we don't do anything about the _____, God _____.

8. The _____ member of the Body of Christ has just as much _____ over the devil as any other member.

9. Before Jesus ascended into Heaven, He _____ His authority to the Church.

10. Authority has nothing to do with _____.

Multiple-Choice Questions

1. Man was never made to be a slave. Instead, God intended that man
   a. Would amass a great fortune so the Gospel would be spread.
   b. Would reign as a king under God.
   c. Would become an intellectual genius who would confound many.
   d. Would be as wise as Solomon.

2. What does it mean that man was created in the image and likeness of God (Gen. 1:26)?
   a. Man was created in the same class of being as God.
   b. Man can stand in the presence of God without any consciousness of inferiority.
   c. Man was made a littler lower than Elohim.
   d. All of the above

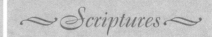

Scriptures

EPHESIANS 3:14–15

14 For this cause I bow my knees unto the Father of our Lord Jesus Christ,

15 Of whom the whole family in heaven and earth is named.

God made you in His image. He made you in His likeness. He made you in the same class of being that He is Himself.

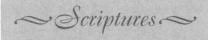

The Bible says we walk by faith and not by sight. By faith—that's the way we possess our Promised Land.

~ Scriptures ~

JOHN 5:26

26 As the Father hath life in himself; so hath he given to the Son to have life in himself.

3. In John 10:10 Jesus said He came so we might have "life." What kind of "life" was He talking about?

a. *Zoe* life, or the very life and nature of God. Man forfeited this "life" in the Garden of Eden but regained it through Christ.

b. A life filled with an abundance of things (cars, boats, and so forth)

c. Having great common sense and a good business sense so whatever you do prospers

d. Having a great family life with several children and many grandchildren

4. What is the God-kind of faith?

a. Faith that is developed through fasting and praying

b. Faith that comes after you memorize most of the Bible

c. Faith that believes in your heart and says with your mouth

d. Both a and b

5. Through the New Birth, you became a part of God's family. The New Birth is also an incarnation. Which answer below best describes the incarnation of God in your life as a born-again Christian?

a. God's life, God's love, and God's light have come into my spirit being. These enable me to be victorious in all areas of my life.

b. The *only* thing the Holy Spirit living inside me guarantees is that I will go to Heaven when I die.

c. Although the Holy Spirit lives inside me, it is normal that I struggle in my daily life.

d. When the Holy Spirit lives inside me, it's like putting a mark on me. This is done so the devil knows he's not supposed to mess with God's kids.

Personal Reflection Questions

1. Do you quickly exercise your authority in Christ in every situation? If not, what can you do to remember to use your authority during adverse times? Is there anything you can do so you automatically exercise your authority every time?

2. Do you feel as though you are "far above all principality, and power, and might, and dominion" (Eph. 1:21)? Do you view situations in your life from a heavenly vantage point? If not, what can you do to see things from God's perspective?

3. Kenneth E. Hagin said that unless believers do something about the devil, nothing will be done. Do you agree with this statement? Why? Now that you are studying your authority as a believer, are you enforcing God's promises in your life?

4. In Mark 16:17, we see that believers are to cast out devils. Have you ever had to cast a devil out of someone? If yes, what happened? If no, how do you think you would react to a demonic manifestation? What can you do so you always react with authority over demons instead of reacting in fear?

5. What does being made in the image of God mean to you? How should this affect your life? Do you fully understand what is available to you? With God residing in you, how should you live your life?

6. Faith will work in your life positively as well as negatively. When it comes to faith, do you operate more in the negative realm or in the positive? In other words, do you expect more bad things to happen to you than good things? What can you do so your faith *always* causes adversity to leave or turn around?

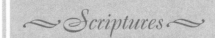

Scriptures

JOHN 1:1–4

1 In the beginning was the Word, and the Word was with God, and the Word was God.

2 The same was in the beginning with God.

3 All things were made by him; and without him was not any thing made that was made.

4 In him was life; and the life was the light of men.

Man was never made a slave. God never intended that man should be a slave to sin, bad habits, sickness, or anything that binds. Man was made to reign as a king under God.

God gave Adam dominion over the work of His hands. God made Adam His understudy, His king to rule over everything that had life.

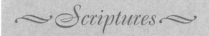

~Scriptures~

I PETER 5:8–9

8 Be sober, be vigilant; because your adversary the devil, as a roaring lion, walketh about, seeking whom he may devour.

9 Whom resist stedfast in the faith, knowing that the same afflictions are accomplished in your brethren that are in the world.

7. How should the *zoe* life of God dwelling in your spirit impact your life? Is it doing that? What does the "God-kind of life" mean to you?

8. Review the scriptures in this lesson. Which one speaks to you the most? Why?

9. Read the quotes in this lesson. Which one is the most meaningful to you? Why?

10. What is one truth you learned from this lesson that you can apply to your life? How will it enhance your life?

BONUS MATERIAL

Born to Raze Hell

Because of Jesus, Christians everywhere can live in victory. But if Jesus had only died on the cross and not been resurrected from the dead, we would not be redeemed. Thank God, He *was* raised from the dead.

Not only was Jesus raised from the dead, He also ascended to Heaven. Hebrews 9:12 says that it was by His own blood that He entered into the heavenly Holy of Holies to obtain eternal redemption for mankind. If Christ had not sat down at the right hand of God, the redemption process would not have been completed. It's through Jesus' death, burial, resurrection, ascension, *and* seating at the right hand of the Father that Satan and his demons were completely defeated and stripped of their power.

Moffatt's translation of First Corinthians 2:6 calls Satan and his demonic forces *"the dethroned Powers who rule this world."*

You may wonder why demons are able to dominate so many people if they've been dethroned. The answer is quite simple: the world doesn't know this. They think the devil is all-powerful.

Christians who know who they are in Christ and who are also doers of the Word know that the devil is defeated. And they don't allow him to dominate them. It's impossible for the devil to rule Christians when they enforce Jesus' victory in their lives.

Many years ago a minister pulled into a service station to get some gas. At that time, gas stations had full-service pumps and self-serve pumps. This minister pulled into the full-service section.

When the attendant began pumping his gas, the minister noticed that he had tattooed on his arm "Born to Raise Hell." The word *raise* means "to cause to come forth; to exalt; to increase." This man was proclaiming, "I was born to exalt hell." Christians, on the other hand, are meant to *raze* hell. *Raze* means "to demolish; to destroy; to utterly remove."

Jesus said in John 14:12, *"He that believeth on me, the works that I do shall he do also."* Christians are supposed to be doing the same works Jesus did. He destroyed the works of the devil, and it's up to us to enforce Satan's defeat.

Jesus went on to say in John 14:13, *"Whatsoever ye shall ask in my name, that will I do."* People have thought that He was talking in this verse about prayer, but He wasn't. The Greek word translated "ask" also means "demand." Jesus was saying, "I'll do whatever you *demand* in My Name." We're not demanding something of God; we're demanding that the devil bow his knee to the Name of Jesus.

Peter and John understood this. On their way to the Temple, they saw a crippled man at the Gate Beautiful begging for alms. Peter looked at the man and said, *"Silver and gold have I none;*

Scriptures

JAMES 4:7

7 Submit yourselves therefore to God. Resist the devil, and he will flee from you.

JOHN 10:10

10 The thief cometh not, but for to steal, and to kill, and to destroy: I am come that they might have life, and that they might have it more abundantly.

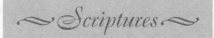

Scriptures

EPHESIANS 1:18–23

18 The eyes of your understanding being enlightened; that ye may know what is the hope of his calling, and what the riches of the glory of his inheritance in the saints,

19 And what is the exceeding greatness of his power to us-ward who believe, according to the working of his mighty power,

20 Which he wrought in Christ, when he raised him from the dead, and set him at his own right hand in the heavenly places,

21 Far above all principality, and power, and might, and dominion, and every name that is named, not only in this world, but also in that which is to come:

22 And hath put all things under his feet, and gave him to be the head over all things to the church,

23 Which is his body, the fulness of him that filleth all in all.

but such as I have give I thee: In the name of Jesus Christ of Nazareth rise up and walk" (Acts 3:6).

Peter demanded in Jesus' Name, and a man who had never walked began walking and leaping and praising God! Peter was *razing* hell. He was demanding that the devil remove his grip from this crippled man.

The Apostle Paul had a similar experience. One time he was preaching the Gospel in Lystra when he perceived that a lame man in the crowd had faith to be healed. Paul said to the man, *"Stand upright on thy feet. And* [the lame man] *leaped and walked"* (Acts 14:10). Paul was razing hell. He was demolishing the works of the devil.

Christians today can do the same thing. We can demand of the devil that we live in divine health and that our needs be abundantly met. We can lay hands on the sick and demand that sickness leave. God promises He will do whatever we ask in Jesus' Name. In doing so, we are *razing*, or demolishing, the works of the devil on the earth!

(*Editor's Note: This article has been adapted from a sermon Kenneth E. Hagin preached on February 17, 1997, at* Winter Bible Seminar.)

The Believer's Authority
Study Guide

Lesson Six

Lesson Overview

Under the Old Covenant, the death of a spotless lamb was the penalty for sin. This sacrifice had to be made year after year. Under the New Covenant, Jesus' death on the cross paid the sin penalty—once and for all—for all mankind. When He emerged from hell, Jesus brought with Him the keys of hell and death (Rev. 1:18).

Physical death is still an enemy. It will be the last enemy to be put underfoot (1 Cor. 15:26). We will not live forever in our physical bodies. But there will come a day when our bodies will be changed. In the twinkling of an eye, we will be clothed with incorruption and will put on immortality. Until that time, we have only limited power over death.

Satan has been stripped of all the power he once had. One way we enforce the devil's defeat is found in Matthew 18:18. It says that whatever we bind on earth will be bound in Heaven and whatever we loose on earth shall be loosed in Heaven.

All too often, Christians haven't used their authority. They've allowed the devil to get a foothold in many areas. They're waiting on God to do something, and He's waiting on them. Heaven promises to back us up in what we refuse and what we allow. Unfortunately, we've allowed a lot of things to happen that we shouldn't have. That's why many Christians are in the situations they're in. Until we use our Matthew 18:18 authority, God won't do anything.

Fill-in-the-Blank Questions

1. _____ formulated the plan of redemption.

2. Death is the penalty for _____.

3. The last enemy that will be put underfoot is _____.

4. Romans 5:17 is talking about _____ death.

5. We are to _____ with Christ right now.

6. When we were born again, the very _____ _____ _____ was imparted into our spirits.

7. Not only have we been adopted into the family of God, but our _____ have been _____.

We are in the family of God—not by adoption only, but by an actual birth of our spirits.

~Scriptures~

I JOHN 3:2

2 Beloved, now are we the sons of God, and it doth not yet appear what we shall be: but we know that, when he shall appear, we shall be like him; for we shall see him as he is.

8. In the New Birth, we have more than just the forgiveness of sins. We have been brought into _____ with God.

9. God took something of Himself—His Spirit—and put it _____ man.

10. We are _____ of God.

Multiple-Choice Questions

1. On the basis of what Jesus did on the cross, God is able to

    a. Redeem us from spiritual death and sin.

    b. Impart His nature to us.

    c. Adopt us as His children and give us eternal life.

    d. All of the above

2. What does it mean to be the "temple of the living God" (2 Cor. 6:16)?

    a. Since God dwells in us, we must adorn ourselves with ornate jewelry and expensive clothing.

    b. Christians are the dwelling place of God on the earth.

    c. The Holy Spirit can dwell in us as long as we don't sin. The moment we sin, the Holy Spirit leaves.

    d. Since we are the temple of God, we don't have to go to church. "Church" is anywhere we are.

Scriptures

I CORINTHIANS 6:19

19 What? know ye not that your body is the temple of the Holy Ghost which is in you, which ye have of God, and ye are not your own?

The incarnation that God has given through the New Birth has bestowed upon us the authority that was lost in the Garden of Eden.

The perfect will of God is for us to live out our full length of time down here without sickness and without disease, and to fall asleep in Jesus.

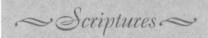

Scriptures

2 CORINTHIANS 6:16

16 And what agreement hath the temple of God with idols? for ye are the temple of the living God; as God hath said, I will dwell in them, and walk in them; and I will be their God, and they shall be my people.

3. When are we able to partake of our inheritance in Christ (Col. 1:12)?

   a. If we are ever able to live completely sin-free, we will be able to partake of our inheritance.

   b. Only mature Christians are fully able to partake of their inheritance.

   c. We partake of our inheritance by faith and can begin enjoying it the moment we are born again.

   d. We will receive our inheritance in Christ when we pass from this life and enter Heaven.

4. Is there anything wrong with singing songs that aren't entirely scriptural?

   a. No. You are simply expressing your feelings.

   b. When you sing songs like this, you tear yourself out of righteousness and put yourself into the realm of death.

   c. It's the beat of the music that you have to watch out for—not the words.

   d. Both a and c

5. Because man was created in the image and likeness of God, he could:

   a. Stand in God's presence without any consciousness of inferiority.

   b. Create new planets by speaking them into existence.

   c. Become all knowing by praying a long time in tongues.

   d. Both b and c

Personal Reflection Questions

1. Are you convinced that whatever you bind on earth is bound in Heaven? How do you know that Heaven will back you up when you use your authority? Give examples of times you have used your authority to bind something on earth. What happened?

2. Which is more important: the Word of God or the Holy Spirit? Why? What are the dangers of getting out beyond the Word of God?

3. What does having eternal life mean to you? Are you walking in eternal life? What can you do to experience right now the kind of life that God has provided for you?

4. What does being a son or daughter of God mean to you? What are some of the rights and privileges you have as a child of God? Are you experiencing the benefits of being God's child? If not, what can you do to receive everything God has for you?

5. You are the temple of the Holy Spirit (1 Cor. 6:19; 2 Cor. 6:16). What does it mean to you to be the dwelling place of God? Are you drawing on the Holy Spirit in all areas of your life? If not, what can you do to be more aware of the Holy Spirit's presence in your life?

6. Are you afraid of the devil? If you are, why? Since Jesus defeated the devil on the cross (Col. 2:15), what steps can you take to enforce His victory in your life?

7. Do you ever feel as though you have a spiritual inferiority complex—that you are hopeless and helpless when trials come? If so, why do you feel inferior? What can you do to change this?

8. Review the scriptures in this lesson. Which one speaks to you the most? Why?

Scriptures

I JOHN 4:4

4 Ye are of God, little children, and have overcome them: because greater is he that is in you, than he that is in the world.

I began to see that God is bigger. He's bigger than blood disease. He's bigger than leukemia. Hallelujah, He's greater than cancer!

9. Read the quotes in this lesson. Which one is the most meaningful to you? Why?

10. What is one truth you learned from this lesson that you can apply to your life? How will it enhance your life?

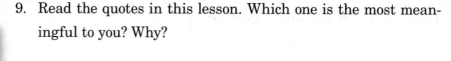

BONUS MATERIAL

For Us—With Us—In Us

In the New Testament God maintains three relations toward the believer. First, God is *for* us. Romans 8:31 says, *"What shall we then say to these things? If God be FOR us, who can be against us?"* If we're not careful, we can forget the Bible is so and that God is for us.

With God on our side, we are guaranteed success. God is not a failure. When we know that He is for us, we can be utterly fearless, no matter how dark the situation or how difficult the problem. We can be sure of this: God has the ability, the power, and the answer to put us over.

Sometimes people miss it and sin. But God is for us, even when we miss it. John was not writing to sinners when he wrote, *"If we confess our sins, he is faithful and just to forgive us our sins, and to cleanse us from all unrighteousness"* (1 John 1:9). God wants to help us and restore us when we miss it. He wants to lift us up even when we stumble and fall.

Proverbs 24:16 says, *"A just man falleth seven times, and riseth up again."* If we've fallen or failed in an area, we can't just lie there. We must get up, repent, and go on with God. He *will* forgive us.

I believe my God is bigger than the devil and all of his cohorts. And I believe that God is in me!

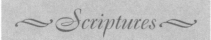

Scriptures

COLOSSIANS 1:14

14 In whom we have redemption through his blood, even the forgiveness of sins.

With Us

Thank God He is *for* us. We don't have to experience defeat when the great unseen One is *for* us. But He is also *with* us. In John 14:23 we read, *"Jesus answered and said unto him, If a man love me, he will keep my words: and my Father will love him, and we will come unto him, and make our abode WITH him."*

Our abode, or home, is the place where we live. Jesus said that *we*—speaking of Himself and God—would make their abode, or home, inside of us. When we're conscious that God is *with* us in all of life's circumstances and difficulties, it will buoy up our faith. We will *know* that God is with us.

In Us

God goes one step further. He is not only *for* us, and *with* us, but He is also *in* us! Ephesians 2:22 says, *"In whom ye also are builded together FOR AN HABITATION OF GOD THROUGH THE SPIRIT."*

God has made His home *in* our bodies! First Corinthians 6:19 says, *"What? know ye not that your body is the temple of the Holy Ghost which is in you, which ye have of God, and ye are not your own?"*

When we accept Jesus as our Lord and Savior, we no longer belong to ourselves. We become the temple of the Holy Spirit. God has made His home in our bodies!

Unfortunately, many Christians are not conscious of this, nor do they really believe it. If they believed that God dwelt in them, they would not talk about their lack of power or ability. There is no lack in God, and since He dwells in us, we should not have any lack either.

Scriptures

COLOSSIANS 1:12–13
(Amplified)

12 Giving thanks to the Father, Who has qualified and made us fit to share the portion which is the inheritance of the saints (God's holy people) in the Light.

13 [The Father] has delivered and drawn us to Himself out of the control and the dominion of darkness and has transferred us into the kingdom of the Son of His love.

God is able to impart unto us—unto our spirits— His very nature.

> David was just a kid of a boy, but he measured that giant, Goliath, by the size of God.

Second Corinthians 6:16 says, *"Ye are the temple of the living God; as God hath said, I will dwell in them, and walk in them; and I will be their God, and they shall be my people."* Why does God live in us? To put us over and help us.

The first three verses of First John chapter 4 talk about demons and evil spirits. The fourth verse begins by saying, *"Ye are of God, little children, and have overcome them. . . ."* "Them" refers to the devil and his cohorts. Through Christ, we have overcome all demonic forces. How? This verse goes on to tell us: *". . . because greater is he that is IN* [us], *than he that is in the world."*

The Greater One—the One Who overcame the devil and his demonic forces lives in us! How big is the Greater One? He's greater than the devil. He's greater than demons and evil spirits. He's greater than sin, sickness, and disease. He's greater than any force or power that tries to come against us!

We let the Greater One dominate our lives by allowing His Word to dominate us. That's why James tells us to be doers of the Word and not hearers only (James 1:22). Scripture says that when we are *only* hearers of the Word, we delude ourselves.

We just need to act as if the Word of God is so—because it is. But if we don't know the Word, we're at a disadvantage. We can't act on what we don't know. When we're full of the Word and incline our ears to what it says, then we'll know what to do in any situation. It's doing the Word, or acting as if it is true, that brings God's blessings in our lives.

When God is *for* us, who can be against us (Rom. 8:31)? And because God is *with* us, He will never forsake us. He will be with us to the end of the world (Matt. 28:20). The Greater One dwells *in* us (1 John 4:4) and will put us over and make us a success in life.

(Editor's Note: This article has been adapted from a message Kenneth E. Hagin preached at a building dedication at Word of Life Christian Center in Las Vegas, Nevada, March 27, 1994.)

The Believer's Authority
Study Guide

Lesson Seven

Instructions

- Read chapter 7, "The Weapons of Our Warfare," from the textbook *The Believer's Authority: Legacy Edition*.

- Listen to the message "Reigning Through Righteousness" from the *Reigning in Life as a King* audio series.

- Work through this lesson.

Lesson Overview

In Ephesians chapter 6 the Apostle Paul tells us, "Be strong in the Lord and in His mighty power" (v. 10). How do we do that? By putting on the whole armor of God. Paul then goes on to list six pieces of armor for us to use in our fight against the devil. Each piece symbolizes a spiritual truth that protects us in our ministry of authority.

When we begin exercising our authority in Christ, we become marked men and women. Satan and his demonic forces don't like it when we use our authority and begin doing the works of Jesus. We are going into their territory and are disrupting their system, and they will do everything they can to stop us. That's why their attacks can seem unrelenting. They will attack us in one area, and when we begin to gain ground, they will attack us in another area.

I always just believed that if the Bible told me to do something, I could do it.

~ Scriptures ~

JOHN 17:20–21

20 Neither pray I for these alone, but for them also which shall believe on me through their word;

21 That they all may be one; as thou, Father, art in me, and I in thee, that they also may be one in us: that the world may believe that thou hast sent me.

But if we will just stand firm, the devil has no choice but to bow to the authority of Christ. If we'll refuse to back down regarding who we are in Christ, and if we'll continue to use our authority, the enemy cannot defeat us.

Fill-in-the-Blank Questions

1. The very thought of reigning also carries the thought of _____ and having _____.

2. Most Christians today are not ruling and reigning in life, because they haven't been _____ to do so.

3. The devil will do everything he can to get you to _____ _____ from your authority.

4. Christians have been _____ with everything they need to _____ the devil.

5. In Ephesians chapter 6, the shield of faith is a _____ for the body and represents our _____ _____ under the blood of Christ.

6. The _____ of the Spirit, which is the Word of God, is our only _____ weapon.

7. The helmet of salvation refers to the _____ of salvation.

8. Our feet are shod with the Gospel of peace. This is a _____ ministry _____ the Word of God.

9. The girdle of truth represents a _____
_____ of God's Word.

10. The breastplate of righteousness has a twofold application: Jesus is our _____, and we put Him on first. It also shows our _____ to the _____.

Multiple-Choice Questions

1. Which of the following can you *not* grow in?

   a. Faith

   b. Righteousness

   c. Knowledge of the Word of God

   d. Your walk with the Lord

2. An advocate is:

   a. A champion of a cause.

   b. An enthusiastic supporter.

   c. One who pleads the case of another.

   d. A person who professes absolute belief in another person.

3. What kind of standing do Christians have with God?

   a. Christians have the same standing with God that Jesus Christ Himself has.

   b. As long as Christians never sin, they have the same standing with God that Christ has.

   c. Because mankind was born in sin, no one can attain complete right standing with God.

   d. As long as a Christian's heart doesn't condemn him, he has the same standing with God that Christ has.

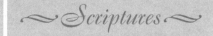

~Scriptures~

JOHN 17:22–23

22 And the glory which thou gavest me I have given them; that they may be one, even as we are one:

23 I in them, and thou in me, that they may be made perfect in one; and that the world may know that thou hast sent me, and hast loved them, as thou hast loved me.

You can't grow in righteousness. You can't have any more right standing with God than what you have right now.

> [Understanding your righteousness in Christ] means that when you stand in the presence of the devil and his works, you don't have a sense of defeat; you have a sense of mastery!

4. As Christians, where are we to reign?

   a. We can only reign in our families.

   b. We will reign with Christ in the millennium.

   c. We should leave reigning to the Lord. It's His responsibility.

   d. We are to reign in this life as well as in the millennium.

5. What enables us to reign with Christ?

   a. Having a firm grasp of spiritual warfare

   b. Reaching a certain level of spiritual perfection (1 Cor. 2:6)

   c. Receiving abundance of grace and the gift of righteousness (Rom. 5:17)

   d. Understanding what spiritual mapping is and praying against the forces of darkness that control a city

Personal Reflection Questions

1. Do you use the spiritual armor that God has provided for you? If not, what can you do to take advantage of that armor? How will spiritual armor enable you to be victorious over the devil?

2. How effective are you in using God's Word as the sword of the Spirit? What are some of the ways you have used the Word to stop the devil in his tracks? What advice would you give others on how to use God's Word effectively?

3. Do you understand that you are the righteousness of God in Christ? What do you do when you miss the mark and sin? Are you able to confess your sin and move on with God? Or do you shrink back from His presence? If you do shrink back, how can you better understand that when you repent, you are forgiven and washed clean?

4. What does reigning in life mean to you? How do you feel about your responsibility to reign in this life? Have you ever tried turning something over to the Lord and letting Him reign over that area? How did that work out? What can *you* do to become more effective in reigning?

5. Have you ever thought you were being humble by having a low opinion of yourself? Why is that way of thinking wrong? Why do you think some people work at trying to become righteous?

6. Do you feel as though you have mastery over the devil? If your answer is no, what can you do to always remember that the devil has been defeated and is under your feet? Have you ever allowed the devil to dominate you? What can you do so this doesn't happen again?

7. What does it mean to you that Jesus is seated at the right hand of God? Is there anything more that Jesus can do for mankind? If He rested from His works, who is going to enforce His will on the earth? What are you doing about this?

8. Review the scriptures in this lesson. Which one speaks to you the most? Why?

9. Read the quotes in this lesson. Which one is the most meaningful to you? Why?

10. What is one truth you learned from this lesson that you can apply to your life? How will it enhance your life?

~ *Scriptures* ~

I JOHN 2:1–2

1 My little children, these things write I unto you, that ye sin not. And if any man sin, we have an advocate with the Father, Jesus Christ the righteous: 2 And he is the propitiation for our sins: and not for ours only, but also for the sins of the whole world.

Not even Jesus Christ Himself has any better standing with God than I do and you do.

> What are you going to do when you don't feel anything? You're going to act like the Bible is so, because it is so. The Bible isn't so just when you FEEL like it is. It's so all the time.

BONUS MATERIAL

God Is *in* Me!

One of the most tremendous facts—and not theories—of God's Word is that when we were born again, we were made new creatures in Christ (2 Cor. 5:17). God recreated us in His own image. In doing so, He did not make us unrighteous men and women who cannot stand in His presence. No, we are sons and daughters of God who can come boldly to His throne of grace (Heb. 4:16).

God sent Jesus to the earth as an incarnation. Jesus took flesh upon Himself. He was a God-man. He was first God and second a human being. In other words, Jesus Christ was a divine human being. We who are born again are children of God. We live in the realm of humanity. But if we are born of God, then we are of God. We are carriers of God on the earth. In essence, we are human divine beings.

No wonder John wrote, *"Ye are OF God, little children"* (1 John 4:4). In both the Old and New Testaments, long lists of genealogies are recorded. Many times we just skip over these passages because the names are hard to pronounce. Today though, we can write our genealogy in four little words: *I am of God!*

In First John 4:4 the apostle went on to say that we *"have overcome them: because greater is he that is in* [us]*, than he that is in the world."* Notice the words *"have overcome them."* What is it we have overcome? The answer is found in the first three verses of First John chapter 4. We have overcome all demonic powers.

John didn't say we're *going* to overcome those powers. He said we *have* overcome them. When Jesus took our place on the cross and overcame Satan and all the forces of hell, it was marked down that *we* overcame the devil! That means we don't have to ask God to help us get victory over the devil. Victory already belongs to us!

We're overcomers not because of how rich or poor we are, or because of how pretty or ugly we are, or because of our family pedigree. We are victorious because the Greater One is in us. If God is in us, then His ability is also in us. And since He's in us, His nature is in us. His love is in us. His wisdom is in us. His strength is in us. *All that He is, is in us!*

To take advantage of what already belongs to us, we should say over and over every day, "God is in me." Some people feel that saying this is sacrilegious. But Scripture tells us this is so. Second Corinthians 6:16 says, *"Ye are the temple of the living God; as God hath said, I will dwell in them, and walk in them; and I will be their God, and they shall be my people."*

Whenever we face what looks like an impossible situation, we simply need to say, "God is in me. God's ability is mine. God's strength is mine. God's health is mine. God's success is mine. I'm a winner. I'm a conqueror. I'm a success!"

So many times in Christendom, believers have thought, "If I can give up this or that and become really spiritual, then I will have arrived." But it's not a matter of giving up something; it's a matter of taking on what already belongs to us. All the benefits of redemption are ours to enjoy. The promises of God belong to us because of redemption, not because of any sacrifice we make.

Let's get a picture of who we are in Christ and start ruling and reigning over evil spirits, demons, sickness, disease, and anything else that tries to defeat us. It's our God-given right to reign over them. They shouldn't dominate us; we should dominate them.

When the devil raises his head against us, he's not coming against us—he's coming against God. Can God be conquered? Absolutely not! Since we are joined to the Lord as one spirit, there

---

~ *Scriptures* ~

EPHESIANS 6:10–11

10 Finally, my brethren, be strong in the Lord, and in the power of his might.

11 Put on the whole armour of God, that ye may be able to stand against the wiles of the devil.

The devil realizes he cannot hold in bondage a believer who knows his authority in Christ Jesus.

is no power on earth that can conquer us. This is why we are able to reign victoriously in life. God is in us!

(*Editor's Note: This article has been adapted from messages Kenneth E. Hagin preached at* Campmeeting *on July 31, 1975, and at the* Spring Satellite Seminar *on April 20, 1988.*)

If believers take advantage of the spiritual armor provided for them, the enemy cannot defeat them.

The Believer's Authority
Study Guide

Lesson Eight

Instructions

- Read chapter 8, "Authority Over Demon Spirits, Not Human Wills," from the textbook *The Believer's Authority: Legacy Edition*.

- Listen to the message "Reigning in Life as a King" from the *Reigning in Life as a King* audio series.

- Work through this lesson.

Lesson Overview

Sometimes people's physical conditions don't respond to prayer and the laying on of hands because evil spirits are involved. This in no way means they are possessed by devils, but they can be oppressed by them. In situations like this, the evil spirit must be dealt with first. The individual will then be able to receive healing. We have authority over demons as far as our lives and the lives of our families are concerned. We *do not* have authority over people in general. We can't cast demons out of people we pass by on the street or casually come in contact with. Their wills are involved. If they don't want to be set free, we can't exercise authority over the devil in them. On the other hand, if they want to be free and they give us permission to exercise authority in their lives, we can do so.

The Word of God is God speaking to me.

~Scriptures~

ROMANS 8:11

11 If the Spirit of him

that raised up Jesus

from the dead

dwell in you,

he that raised up Christ

from the dead

shall also quicken

your mortal bodies

by his Spirit that

dwelleth in you.

Fill-in-the-Blank Questions

1. We have _____ over demons but not over another person's _____.

2. If someone doesn't want to be _____, we can't _____ them.

3. It is within our authority to _____ the power of the devil over a _____ _____ life.

4. We know from the _____ that we have spiritual authority, but we must depend on the _____ _____ to help us in ministering that authority. We can't do it by ourselves.

5. If we _____ to exercise our authority to see if it will work, it won't work.

6. When people are in places like a church conference where faith is high or where the gifts of the Spirit are in operation, it's _____ for them to be healed.

7. It's when a person doesn't have a solid _____ _____ _____ that the devil can easily put sickness back on them after they have been healed.

8. The Bible differentiates between casting out devils and healing the sick. In some cases a _____ must be cast out before a person can be _____.

9. We can take authority over volatile situations we are in, and the spirit behind them has to _____ us.

10. We are told to _____ the devil. If we don't, someone else can't _____ the devil for us.

Multiple-Choice Questions

1. Why is it that some Christians have not realized what belongs to them in Christ?

    a. They don't know what the Scriptures say.

    b. They are listening to what others say.

    c. They are following religious traditions.

    d. All of the above

2. How are we saved?

    a. By doing good works

    b. Through right conduct

    c. By grace through faith

    d. All of the above

3. What happens when we become new creatures in Christ (2 Cor. 5:17)?

    a. Our spirit being is made new.

    b. An amazing transformation takes place in our body. For instance, if we were bald, hair begins to grow!

    c. Our entire thought process changes. We now think in line with biblical truths.

    d. No matter how old we are, we suddenly look 10 years younger.

4. Why does it seem as if the devil doesn't flee when we resist him (James 4:7)?

    a. Demons don't have to leave places where they have controlled people for generations.

    b. We haven't firmly stood our ground.

    c. We haven't been militant enough in our combat against the devil.

    d. Both a and c

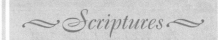

~Scriptures~

I CORINTHIANS 3:16

16 Know ye not that ye are the temple of God, and that the Spirit of God dwelleth in you?

The very fact that [God] said "reign as kings" leaves the thought or impression that we're to be on top in life and not on the bottom.

5. What does Satan's defeat mean to mankind?

   a. If a person is attacked with *any* kind of sickness or disease, that person can be healed.

   b. Lack and poverty no longer have to dominate our lives.

   c. We don't have to fear any kind of danger. God is there to protect us.

   d. All of the above

Personal Reflection Questions

1. Did you ever use the authority you have in Christ on behalf of a family member? What were the results? Have you ever tried to exercise your authority on behalf of someone you did not know? What happened?

2. Have you ever tried to act on God's Word and had it not work for you? Why do you think it didn't work? What can you do differently the next time? How can you build your faith in that area?

3. Why do you think some people lose their healing? Have you ever lost your healing? What can you do to keep your healing?

4. What does it mean to be the temple of the Holy Spirit? How has your life changed since you were born again—since God moved inside you? Are you living in more victory? If not, why do you think that's the case?

5. Do you feel that the Greater One dwells in you? If you don't, how can you have a deeper revelation of this? If you do feel He dwells in you, what have you experienced as a result of His indwelling presence?

You need to realize that the New Birth is not only a new birth and a rebirth of our human spirits; it is actually an incarnation. God Himself comes to live inside us.

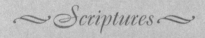

Scriptures

I CORINTHIANS 15:27

27 He hath put all things under his feet. But when he saith all things are put under him, it is manifest that he is excepted, which did put all things under him.

6. Are you seated in heavenly places with Christ? Why do you think so? What does it mean to you to sit in this place of authority?

7. How is your fight of faith coming along? What do you do when the devil roars like a lion in your life? What can you do so you don't shrink back when fiery darts hit your shield of faith?

8. Review the scriptures in this lesson. Which one speaks to you the most? Why?

9. Read the quotes in this lesson. Which one is the most meaningful to you? Why?

10. What is one truth you learned from this lesson that you can apply to your life? How will it enhance your life?

BONUS MATERIAL

True Spiritual Warfare

From the early days of the Church, Christians have engaged in spiritual warfare. By looking at the examples that were set for us in the Bible, we can be successful in our stand against the devil today.

Acts chapter 3 records the story of a lame man who was healed when Peter and John were on their way to the Temple. Every day the man sat at the entrance of the gate called Beautiful begging for money. One day he asked Peter and John for alms as they were

Scriptures

2 CORINTHIANS 6:18

18 And [I] will be a Father unto you, and ye shall be my sons and daughters, saith the Lord Almighty.

The fight of faith is to believe what the Bible says.

~Scriptures~

EPHESIANS 2:4–6

4 But God, who is rich in

mercy, for his great love

wherewith he loved us,

5 Even when we were

dead in sins,

hath quickened us

together with Christ,

(by grace ye are saved;)

6 And hath raised us up

together, and made us

sit together

in heavenly places

in Christ Jesus.

passing by. Peter said, *"Silver and gold have I none; but such as I have give I thee: In the name of Jesus Christ of Nazareth rise up and walk"* (Acts 3:6). This man, who had been lame from his mother's womb, immediately jumped to his feet and began walking!

Peter boldly preached Christ to those who were in the Temple. His message so outraged the chief priests and elders that they had Peter and John arrested. Then these leaders commanded the apostles not to preach or teach anymore in the Name of Jesus. After they were released, they went back to their own company and told them what happened.

ACTS 4:24–31

24 And when [the company of disciples] heard that, they lifted up their voice to God with one accord, and said, Lord, thou art God, which hast made heaven, and earth, and the sea, and all that in them is:

25 Who by the mouth of thy servant David hast said, Why did the heathen rage, and the people imagine vain things?

26 The kings of the earth stood up, and the rulers were gathered together against the Lord, and against his Christ.

27 For of a truth against thy holy child Jesus, whom thou hast anointed, both Herod, and Pontius Pilate, with the Gentiles, and the people of Israel, were gathered together,

28 For to do whatsoever thy hand and thy counsel determined before to be done.

29 And now, Lord, behold their threatenings: and grant unto thy servants, that with all boldness they may speak thy word,

30 By stretching forth thine hand to heal; and that signs and wonders may be done by the name of thy holy child Jesus.

31 And when they had prayed, the place was shaken where they were assembled together; and they were all filled with the Holy Ghost, and they spake the word of God with boldness.

Notice that these Christians never dealt with the devil. Instead, they talked to God about how big He was. They brought His Word to Him. It wasn't until verse 29 that they mentioned their problem.

Nowadays people often talk more about the devil than they do God. The way they talk you would think that Jesus didn't do anything when He died, rose from the dead, and spoiled principalities and powers. When people talk so much about the devil, Satan is magnified to a greater degree than what he deserves. What a difference it would make if believers would quit trying to deal with the devil and instead talk to God.

In one church we pastored, a little red-headed lady by the name of Sister Sylvia attended. She could pray Heaven and earth together. My wife and I often asked her to help us pray. Some folks know how to pray, and when you need help, that's who you turn to.

One time one of our church ladies brought her sister, who was insane, to our parsonage. I told my wife, "Let's get Sister Sylvia." When we got back to the parsonage, we didn't begin binding, loosing, and rebuking the devil. No. First, we got over in the Spirit. What do I mean by that? We began praying in other tongues and ministering to the Lord.

For two hours we *did not* deal with or talk to the devil. We didn't even pray for the woman. We just prayed and worshipped God. We prayed with our understanding as best we could. Before long, we were praying in other tongues.

This is where a lot of people miss it. They jump in right away and try to deal with the devil. They first need to talk about God and how big He is. That's what they did in the Book of Acts.

We worshipped God and talked about His bigness. After a while, God started talking to us. The Spirit of God said to me, "Go stand in front of her and say 'Come out of her, thou unclean spirit, in the Name of Jesus.'" When I obeyed the Lord, the woman was gloriously healed!

Some Christians have taken spiritual warfare to a level that is not biblically correct. They scream and yell at the devil at the top of their voices, which is thoroughly unscriptural. There isn't any verse in the entire Bible that tells us to do this. At one time

God through the New Birth moved into us and He lives in us, and we have never mastered that subject.

during the 1970s and 1980s, Christians wore army fatigues and combat boots while they prayed. Others chartered airplanes or rented space on the top floors of skyscrapers. They believed the higher they got in the atmosphere, the better they could "combat" the devil.

Christians who do this are trying to do in the flesh what Jesus has already done in the spirit. We shouldn't be so interested in getting *up* in the heavenlies to deal with evil spirits. We should be interested in praying the power of God *down*.

In Acts 4:31 after Peter, John, and the other believers had prayed, *"the place was shaken where they were assembled together."* Some people get excited when they begin to shake, but wait till the *building* starts shaking!

The Church in its early days was equipped with the same armor that we're equipped with. If we'll follow their example, we'll have the same results. By focusing on the Greater One Who dwells inside us, we will be victorious over every attack of the enemy.

(*Editor's Note: This article has been adapted from a message Kenneth E. Hagin preached at* Winter Bible Seminar *on February 19, 1991.*)

The Believer's Authority
Study Guide

Lesson Nine

Instructions

- Read appendixes 1 and 2 from the textbook *The Believer's Authority: Legacy Edition*.

- Work through this lesson.

Lesson Overview

During His confrontation with the devil in the wilderness, Jesus proved Himself to be Master over the enemy of mankind. He overcame each temptation the devil brought by countering it with the Word of God. Jesus went on to conquer death and destroy the devil's power over mankind. After His resurrection and ascension into Heaven, He handed us His victory.

Through the Name of Jesus, Christians can also become masters over all of Satan's devices, including mental illness. Christians who have been afflicted by mental illness can be set free. Mental illness isn't different from physical illness—the blood of Jesus heals both.

God is ALWAYS speaking
to us through His Word.

~ Scriptures ~

HEBREWS 2:14–15 (ASV)

14 Since then the children

are sharers in flesh and

blood, he also himself in like

manner partook of the

same; that through death

he might bring to nought

him that had the power of

death, that is, the devil;

15 and might deliver all them

who through fear of death

were all their lifetime

subject to bondage.

Fill-in-the-Blank Questions

1. God is always speaking to us through _____
   _____.

2. In the Bible, all _____ recognized Jesus'
   authority and knew Who He was.

3. All Christians need to know how to _____
   Satan the same way Jesus did.

4. The three kinds of death are _____,
   _____, and the _____ _____.

5. Principalities and powers in Colossians 2:15 refer to
   _____ beings.

6. After Jesus crushed Satan and his demonic forces, He handed
   us His _____.

7. Instead of resting in Christ's victory, many Christians are trying to _____ the devil in their own
   _____.

8. Many times we want God to speak to us in _____
   ways, but He is talking to us all the time through His
   _____.

9. Christians have been set free from the law of _____
   and _____.

10. Your _____ is the door to your _____.

Multiple-Choice Questions

1. How can someone be delivered from evil spirits?

   a. Pray and fast for two weeks before laying hands on the individual.

   b. Take the person to a side room and make him vomit up the evil spirit.

   c. Preach the Word—preach deliverance to him.

   d. Scream and yell at the devil at the top of your voice so he knows you mean business. Then you can cast him out.

2. How can you get your prayers answered every time?

   a. Confess "I believe I receive" at least a thousand times after praying.

   b. Abide in the Word of God (John 15:7).

   c. Fast and pray for 40 days.

   d. Call every prayer line you know of.

3. Why can't a born-again, Spirit-filled Christian be possessed by the devil in his or her spirit?

   a. Because according to Second Corinthians 5:17, the Christian is a new creature in Christ.

   b. The Holy Spirit and the devil cannot abide in the same place.

   c. A *mature* believer would have to deny Christ willfully with deliberate forethought before he could ever allow a demon to gain access into his spirit. If a mature believer did deny Christ, he would cease to be a Christian, for the word *Christian* means "Christ-like."

   d. All of the above

~Scriptures~

2 TIMOTHY 4:2

2 Preach the word.

The Word tells us to PREACH deliverance, not PRAY deliverance.

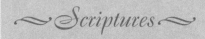

The reason so many Christians have problems with the devil is that they're always trying to defeat him in their own strength.

~Scriptures~

2 CORINTHIANS 2:14–15

14 Now thanks be unto God, which always causeth us to triumph in Christ, and maketh manifest the savour of his knowledge by us in every place.

15 For we are unto God a sweet savour of Christ, in them that are saved, and in them that perish.

4. What can happen if you do not renew your mind with the Word of God?

   a. Your mind will side with your body. Instead of your spirit governing your body through your mind, your body will dominate your spirit through your mind.

   b. You will be a carnal, or body-ruled, Christian.

   c. You won't know or exercise your rightful authority in Christ and will open yourself up to the attacks of the enemy.

   d. All of the above

5. What can you learn from Psalm 23?

   a. The shorter the psalm, the better.

   b. The table the Lord has prepared for us contains everything we need, but we must keep our eyes on the table and not on adverse situations that surround us.

   c. To receive what is on this table, you must be righteous. Your righteousness is determined by your good deeds.

   d. This psalm really isn't relevant today.

Personal Reflection Questions

1. Have you ever wanted God to lead you in a spectacular way? What happened? Why do you feel it is better, or not better, to be led by the still, small voice of the Holy Spirit or through the Word of God?

2. What does it mean to you that Satan has been paralyzed and brought to nothing? How has he been brought to nothing in your life? What can you do to help others understand that the devil has no authority over them?

3. Do you ever feel as though you are trying to defeat the devil in your own strength? Have you ever "declared war on the devil"? Did you win? What can you do to rest in the victory that Christ won for you?

4. What does dominion mean to you? Are you walking in your dominion? If you're not, what can you do to start exercising your authority in Christ?

5. What is the difference between "preaching" deliverance to the captives and "praying" for someone's deliverance? Why is preaching a better way to get some people delivered?

6. Is it possible for someone with mental illness to be delivered? How are mental and physical illness different in regard to being healed or delivered?

7. How is it possible for the devil to gain control of a person's mind? What help is there for a person when this happens? How does renewing your mind help in situations like this?

8. Is it possible to live worry-free? How can you keep from worrying? What scriptures can you stand on to eliminate worry from your life? What are some benefits of not worrying?

9. Review the scriptures in this lesson. Which one speaks to you the most? Why?

10. Read the quotes in this lesson. Which one is the most meaningful to you? Why?

11. What is one truth you learned from this lesson that you can apply to your life? How will it enhance your life?

The peace of God passes our human understanding. God's peace is sort of like the anointing—you can't explain it in human terms.

~Scriptures~

REVELATION 1:17–18 (ASV)

17 Fear not;

I am the first

and the last,

18 and the Living one;

and I was dead,

and behold, I am alive

for evermore,

and I have

the keys of death

and of Hades.

BONUS MATERIAL

Why the Delay?

Nowadays people want everything instantly. However, when it comes to prayer, many times answers don't come right away. What we do from the time we pray until the answer arrives is critical.

Some Christians quickly give up when they experience an obstacle or don't see an answer to their prayer. In their mind, a delay means that God doesn't want them to have what they're praying for. They never stop to think that other forces could be involved.

In the Book of Daniel, we get a glimpse of what can be happening when it seems as if the answers to our prayers are delayed. The children of Israel were in captivity in Babylon and as Daniel was reading the Scriptures, it appeared that their time of captivity should have come to an end. So Daniel began seeking the Lord about what he had read.

In response to Daniel's prayers, God wanted to reveal to him what was about to take place on the earth and what would happen in the future. In the spirit realm, however, demonic forces tried to stop the message from getting through. But finally, after 21 days, an angel appeared to Daniel in a vision.

DANIEL 10:12–13

12 Fear not, Daniel: for from the first day that thou didst set thine heart to understand, and to chasten thyself before thy God, thy words were heard, and I am come for thy words.

13 But the prince of the kingdom of Persia withstood me one and twenty days: but, lo, Michael, one of the chief princes, came to help me; and I remained there with the kings of Persia.

The "prince of the kingdom of Persia" referred to in verse 13 was not an earthly prince. He was a demonic being that ruled the spiritual kingdom of darkness over Persia.

A Heavenly Warfare

The moment Daniel began to pray, war erupted in the heavenlies. Remember what Jesus said in Matthew 18:18: *"Whatsoever ye shall bind on earth shall be bound in heaven: and whatsoever ye shall loose on earth shall be loosed in heaven."* Daniel bound the devil through intercessory prayer. That is not the only way to bind demonic forces, but it is one way.

It's important to note that although Matthew 18:18 talks about heaven, it's not referring to the place where God resides. The Bible actually talks about three heavens. The first heaven is the atmosphere, or the air around us. It's the first heaven that is infested with demons, and the prince of the power of the air rules there. The second heaven is where the stars and planets are, and beyond that is the Heaven of heavens, which is Paradise.

The "heaven" in Matthew 18:18 can't be the Heaven where God resides. There isn't anything in the third Heaven that needs to be bound. No, Matthew 18:18 is referring to the first heaven, or the atmosphere around us. And when we use our authority in Christ, we can stop the actions of the principalities, powers, and rulers of the darkness of this world.

Let Us Pray!

In looking at what happened to Daniel, we can learn two important truths. First, God did not send the angel from Heaven until Daniel prayed. The same is true with you and me. God

God prepares a table BEFORE us—the tables in front of us and the devil's behind us.

doesn't arbitrarily intervene on our behalf. We first have to pray and ask God for whatever it is that we need.

Second, Daniel continued to pray until he received his answer. He kept pressing in to hear from God. If we don't get an answer immediately, that doesn't mean God did not hear us or isn't going to answer us. We simply need to persevere in prayer. And like Daniel, we will receive an answer if we just don't quit.

(Editor's Note: This article has been adapted from a message Kenneth E. Hagin taught during a Spring Satellite Seminar on May 5, 1987.)

The Believer's Authority
Study Guide

Lesson Ten

Instructions

- Read appendixes 3 and 4 from the textbook *The Believer's Authority: Legacy Edition*.

- Work through this lesson.

Lesson Overview

John 15:7 says, *"If ye abide in me [Jesus], and my words abide in you, ye shall ask what ye will, and it shall be done unto you."* The words *you* and *ye* are in this verse five times. This repetition shows us that receiving answered prayer depends more on *us* than it does on God. We are told to put God in remembrance of His Word (Isa. 43:26). When we remind Him of His promises, we are also reminding ourselves of what He said. Charles G. Finney, a renowned 19th-century preacher, often put God in remembrance of His Word. When he held a revival, it was common for nearly every person in that town to get saved. One secret to Finney's success was his prayer life. Finney reminded God of what He said concerning revival. It is imperative that we feed on the Word daily. We need to know what God's Word says regarding what we are praying for.

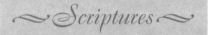

Some of the greatest leadings we have are when we're unconsciously led.

Scriptures

EPHESIANS 6:18

18 Praying always

with all prayer and

supplication in the Spirit,

and watching thereunto

with all perseverance

and supplication

for all saints.

Fill-in-the-Blank Questions

1. Many of God's promises are _____.
   If we want to enjoy the results, we must meet the
   _____.

2. God blotted out our transgressions for _____ sake.
   He did this because He wanted to bless _____.

3. Bringing up past sin is a ploy of the devil to _____ us.

4. The Word gives you _____ and _____ in
   prayer.

5. God wants us to _____ Him of His
   _____ when we pray.

6. We can _____ in prayer on behalf of others in
   the same way Abraham interceded on behalf of Sodom and
   Gomorrah.

7. We should not pray the same way every time we pray. Instead,
   we should be _____ by the _____
   _____ when we pray.

8. Some of the greatest leadings we have are when we are
   _____ led.

9. Christians have a lot more to do with when they _____
   than they think. They can make the _____
   themselves and not let the devil make it for them.

10. God wants us to live a healthy, _____ _____.
    It brings more glory to Him if our _____ isn't
    caused by sickness or accident but by natural means.

Multiple-Choice Questions

1. What happens when we choose to forget our past transgressions in the same way God has forgotten them (Isa. 43:25–26)?

    a. Any guilt vanishes.

    b. We can get away with more because God doesn't remember how many times we've committed the same sin.

    c. We can stand in God's presence with no consciousness of sin.

    d. Both a and c

2. Why should we find scriptures that promise us the things we are praying for?

    a. Knowing the Word gives us authority in prayer.

    b. It helps us memorize scripture, and we should memorize a new verse at least once a month.

    c. Our prayers will sound more impressive.

    d. If we sound more scholarly and eloquent, then others will be able to agree with us better.

3. What must happen for Matthew 18:19 to be an effective prayer?

    a. As long as the prayer ends with "we agree in Jesus' Name," it will be answered, even if one person is not really sure that God will answer the prayer.

    b. The people who are praying must be holding hands. The prayer of agreement won't work if they aren't touching each other by holding hands.

    c. The people praying must agree, or have the same desired outcome, on what they are praying about.

    d. All of the above

God wants us to enjoy LONG LIFE—and for that life to be one of divine health.

Throughout church history, the mighty men of prayer have been those who reminded God of His promises.

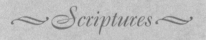

JOHN 15:7

7 If ye abide in me, and my words abide in you, ye shall ask what ye will, and it shall be done unto you.

4. Charles G. Finney once stated that he had experiences in prayer that "alarmed" him. What caused him to be alarmed?

   a. He saw into the spirit realm and could see the spiritual forces that controlled different cities.

   b. He boldly reminded God of what He had said in His Word concerning revival.

   c. He was threatened with jail because he prayed so loudly that he disturbed his neighbors.

   d. Seeing into the spirit realm, he saw thousands upon thousands of people going to hell.

5. Can you plead the case of another person?

   a. You can only plead the case for a person who attends church all the time and who always pays his or her tithes.

   b. Yes, we have a certain amount of authority to plead the case of another person by demanding in prayer what belongs to them.

   c. If you don't know a person, you could plead their case by throwing yourself on the mercy of God.

   d. Both b and c

Personal Reflection Questions

1. What does abiding in Christ and having His words abide in you mean to you? Do you allow "life" to keep you from abiding in the Word of God? If you do, what would it take to change this? What are the benefits of abiding in Christ and having His Word abide in you?

2. Is it God's responsibility to see that your prayers are answered? Why?

3. According to Isaiah 43:25, God blots out our transgressions and no longer remembers our sins. Do you ever struggle because you remember things from your past? What can you do to forget your past mistakes? If other people try to bring your past up to you, what should you say?

4. Charles G. Finney was known for his prayer life. Do you know anyone today who has great results in their prayer life? What can be done to ensure a good prayer life?

5. Have you ever been unconsciously led by the Holy Spirit? What happened? Are you often led this way?

6. Why is it important to find scriptures to back up what you are praying for? How often do you do this? Can you tell a difference between the times you pray according to Scripture and the times you don't?

7. Do you feel Christians have the right to choose the time they go home to be with the Lord? What scriptures support your belief?

8. Review the scriptures in this lesson. Which one speaks to you the most? Why?

9. Read the quotes in this lesson. Which one is the most meaningful to you? Why?

10. What is one truth you learned from this lesson that you can apply to your life? How will it enhance your life?

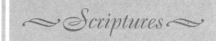 Scriptures

JOHN 14:13

13 And whatsoever ye shall ask in my name, that will I do, that the Father may be glorified in the Son.

If [God's] words don't abide in you, you don't know what to remind Him of. That's the reason we need to get full of the Word.

Scriptures

ISAIAH 43:25–26

25 I, even I, am he
that blotteth out
thy transgressions
for mine own sake,
and will not
remember thy sins.
26 Put me in remembrance:
let us plead together:
declare thou, that thou
mayest be justified.

Contending for the Lost

In writing to the churches throughout Galatia, Paul said, *"My little children, of whom I travail in birth again until Christ be formed in you"* (Gal. 4:19). Paul had already "travailed in birth" for the Galatians to be born again. And now he's continuing to make intercession for their spiritual growth. Although the Galatians had been born again and filled with the Holy Ghost, Christ *had not* been formed in them as He should have been. They were not growing spiritually. Instead of going forward in Christ, they wanted to get back under the confines of the Jewish law.

I believe the reason that too few folks are being saved and that a number of Christian conversions never amount to anything is that not enough travailing prayer or intercession is being made. Isaiah 66:8 says, *"As soon as Zion travailed, she brought forth her children."* Many say that this scripture refers to Israel being reborn as a nation, and of course that truth is there. But I believe it can also apply to the lost. If no travail is made, then there will be no children.

It's certainly true that Jesus said, *"Go ye into all the world, and preach the gospel to every creature"* (Mark 16:15). We must realize that some people will simply believe in Christ after hearing the Gospel message. But there are others who will never be saved unless someone intercedes for them, unless someone travails in prayer for them. We need to know that we can travail in birth, in intercession, for the lost.

When I was holding what we called revival meetings, during the day I set aside time to pray for the night services. Many times while praying, I felt as if I was lost myself. Why? I took that burden upon my own spirit. When that happens, I feel the same way the lost do. I feel the same burden of sin on my conscience that they do.

Through the years people have said to me, "I know I'm saved and filled with the Holy Ghost. But when the altar call is given, such a burden comes on me. I feel as if I'm lost myself. I don't understand it. I feel as if I should go to the altar."

I'd explain to them that they should just sit quietly in their pew and begin interceding for the unsaved in the congregation without disrupting the service. You don't want to pray so loud that people start watching you. When someone disrupts a service in this way, usually the ones who need to respond to the altar call don't. I've seen them get up and leave.

You can pray quietly within yourself. But if you become so burdened that you can't pray quietly, just slip out of the service and go to the prayer room. You can lift your voice out loud in intercession there without disturbing anybody.

In 1939 my wife and I were holding a revival in a little church down in Texas. We only had night services, so every day at 10 o'clock in the morning, we'd pray with the pastor for the evening services. One day as we were praying, I took upon myself the burden of the lost. While I was praying, I cried out, "Lost! I'm lost!" Well, I wasn't lost. I was taking the place of someone who was lost.

I had a vision during that time of prayer. I saw what looked like a river of people flowing over a cliff into a lake of fire. And I tumbled over that cliff right with them. I screamed as I went down into that lake of fire. I cried out, "I'm burning! Water! Ohhh, water!"

When I finished praying, I found out that I had prayed for three hours! I thought it had been only 10 or 15 minutes.

Scriptures

ISAIAH 43:26 (NASB)

26 "Put Me in remembrance, let us argue our case together; state your cause, that you may be proved right."

Find scriptures that promise you the things you're praying for and you'll have a solid foundation for faith.

That night at the revival, I preached only 15 minutes and the power of God fell. I didn't have to ask anybody to come to the altar—they just came. The pastor later told me, "Every unsaved person and backslider in the building got saved!"

Only the Holy Ghost knows who will respond to the Gospel simply by hearing the Word preached, and who will need intercessory prayer made on their behalf. Intercession overpowers the works of the devil, and strongholds can be pulled down. When the devil's works in a person's life are broken, then it's easy to get them saved, because they're willing to give their lives to the Lord.

(*Editor's Note: This article has been adapted from a message Kenneth E. Hagin preached at* Spring Satellite Seminar *on May 6, 1987.*)

Lesson One

Fill-in-the-Blank Questions
1. authority
2. act, automatically
3. cannot, allow
4. truth
5. prayer, God's Word
6. Lord, ourselves
7. in
8. authority
9. exercised, allowed
10. power

Multiple Choice Questions
1. c. The devil will take advantage of their ignorance and dominate their lives.
2. c. The truth of the Word
3. a. The power behind it
4. d. We should look to the Greater One Who dwells in our hearts.
5. b. No, we are only able to exercise authority over spirits, not people.

Lesson Two

Fill-in-the-Blank Questions
1. raised up together
2. waste
3. flee from
4. to run from as if in terror
5. the devil, God
6. God's, our might
7. same authority
8. take, give
9. done, devil
10. dominate

Multiple Choice Questions
1. d. All of the above
2. b. God Himself
3. a. Every born-again believer
4. c. Resist him and use your authority in Christ
5. d. All of the above

Lesson Three

Fill-in-the-Blank Questions
1. place, authority
2. mightiest
3. Heaven, earth, and hell
4. resurrection
5. victory
6. one
7. all
8. greater
9. authority
10. mankind

Multiple Choice Questions
1. b. The believer who knows and acts on his rights, privileges, and authority in Christ can control how a situation turns out.
2. d. All of the above
3. c. God is dependent upon the Church to carry out His commands and exercise authority.
4. a. We are to present our bodies to Him.
5. c. We allow our spirit man to dominate our bodies.

Lesson Four

Fill-in-the-Blank Questions
1. evil spirits
2. today, future
3. born again
4. dominate
5. Jesus, Christians
6. second Adam
7. unbelief, reason
8. demand
9. demand
10. Word, see

Multiple Choice Questions
1. d. All of the above
2. d. All of the above
3. c. Quit talking fear
4. b. The Church today has the same amount of power that the Early Church had.
5. d. All of the above

Lesson Five

Fill-in-the-Blank Questions
1. God, earth
2. stand, flee
3. us, Him
4. Body of Christ
5. above
6. enforce
7. devil, can't
8. least, authority
9. delegated
10. feelings

Multiple Choice Questions
1. b. Would reign as a king under God
2. d. All of the above
3. a. *Zoe* life, or the very life and nature of God
4. c. Faith that believes in your heart and says with you mouth
5. a. God's life, God's love, and God's light have come into your spirit being. These enable me to be victorious in all areas of my life.

Lesson Six

Fill-in-the-Blank Questions
1. God
2. sin
3. death
4. spiritual
5. reign
6. life of God
7. spirits, reborn
8. union
9. into
10. carriers

Multiple Choice Questions
1. d. All of the above
2. b. Christians are the dwelling place of God on the earth.
3. c. We partake of our inheritance by faith, and can begin enjoying it the moment we become born again.
4. b. When you sing songs like this, you tear yourself out of your righteousness and put yourself in the realm of death.
5. a. Stand in God's presence without any consciousness of inferiority.

Lesson Seven

Fill-in-the-Blank Questions
1. ruling, dominion
2. taught
3. back down
4. equipped, overcome
5. covering, complete safety
6. sword, offensive
7. hope
8. faithful, proclaiming
9. clear understanding
10. righteousness, obedience, Word

Multiple Choice Questions
1. b. Righteousness
2. c. One who pleads the case of another.
3. a. Christians have the same standing with God that Jesus Christ Himself has.
4. d. We are to reign in this life, as well as in the millennium.
5. c. Receiving abundance of grace and the gift of righteousness (Rom. 5:17)

Lesson Eight

Fill-in-the-Blank Questions
1. authority, will
2. helped, help
3. break, family member's
4. Bible, Holy Spirit
5. try
6. easy
7. foundation of faith
8. spirit, healed
9. obey
10. resist, resist

Multiple Choice Questions
1. d. All of the above
2. c. By grace through faith
3. a. Our spirit being is made new.
4. b. We haven't firmly stood our ground
5. d. All of the above

Lesson Nine

Fill-in-the-Blank Questions
1. His Word
2. demons
3. master
4. spiritual, physical, second death
5. demonic
6. victory
7. defeat, strength
8. spectacular, Word
9. sin, death
10. mind, heart

Multiple Choice Questions
1. c. Preach the Word—preach deliverance to him.
2. b. Abide in the Word of God (John 15:7)
3. d. All of the above
4. a. All of the above
5. b. The table the Lord has prepared for us contains everything we need, but we must keep our eyes on the table and not on adverse situations that surround us.

Lesson Ten

Fill-in-the-Blank Questions

1. conditional, conditions
2. His, us
3. defeat
4. faith, confidence
5. remind, Word
6. intervene
7. led, Holy Spirit
8. unconsciously
9. die, decision
10. long life, death

Multiple Choice Questions

1. d. Both a and c
   a. Any guilt vanishes.
   c. We can stand in God's presence with no consciousness of sin.
2. a. Knowing the Word gives us authority in prayer.
3. c. The people praying must agree, or have the same desired outcome, on what they are praying about.
4. b. He boldly reminded God of what He had said in His Word concerning revival.
5. d. Both b and c
   b. Yes, we have a certain amount of authority to plead the case of another person by demanding in prayer what belongs to them.
   c. If you don't know a person, you could plead their case by throwing yourself on the mercy of God.

Always on.

For the latest news and information on products, media, podcasts, study resources, and special offers, visit us online 24 hours a day.

rhema.org

Free Subscription!

Call now to receive a free subscription to *The Word of Faith* magazine from Kenneth Hagin Ministries. Receive encouragement and spiritual refreshment from . . .

- *Faith-building articles from Kenneth W. Hagin, Lynette Hagin, Craig W. Hagin, Denise Hagin Burns, and others*

- *"Timeless Teaching" from the archives of Kenneth E. Hagin*

- *Feature articles on prayer and healing*

- *Testimonies of salvation, healing, and deliverance*

- *Children's activity page*

- *Updates on Rhema Bible Training College, Rhema Bible Church, and other outreaches of Kenneth Hagin Ministries*

Subscribe today for your free *Word of Faith*!

1-888-28-FAITH (1-888-283-2484)

rhema.org/wof

OFFER CODE—BKORD:WF

Rhema

Correspondence Bible School

The Rhema Correspondence Bible School is a home Bible study course that can help you in your everyday life!

This course of study has been designed with you in mind, providing practical teaching on prayer, faith, healing, Spirit-led living, and much more to help you live a victorious Christian life!

Flexible

Enroll any time: choose your topic of study;
study at your own pace!

Affordable

Profitable

"The Lord has blessed me through a Rhema Correspondence Bible School graduate. . . . He witnessed to me 15 years ago, and the Lord delivered me from drugs and alcohol. I was living on the streets and then in somebody's tool shed. Now I lead a victorious and blessed life! I now am a graduate of Rhema Correspondence Bible School too! I own a beautiful home. I have a beautiful wife and two children who also love the Lord. The Lord allows me to preach whenever my pastor is out of town. I am on the board of directors at my church and at the Christian school. Thank you, and God bless you and your ministry!"

—D.J., Lusby, Maryland

"Thank you for continually offering Rhema Correspondence Bible School. The eyes of my understanding have been enlightened greatly through the Word of God through having been enrolled in RCBS. My life has forever been changed."

—M.R., Princeton, N.C.

For enrollment information and a course listing, call today!

1-888-28-FAITH (1-888-283-2484)

rhema.org/rcbs

OFFER CODE—BKORD:BRCSC